Colored
YMCA
℃G

Priscilla T Graham

Copyright © 2021 by Priscilla T Graham
All Rights Reserved.
Colored YMCA

ISBN: 978-1-953824-01-1
Printed in the United States of America

All Rights Reserved. No part of this book may be reproduced or transmitted in any form or by any means, electronic or mechanical, including photocopying, recording or any information storage and retrieval system without written permission of the publisher except for brief quotations used in reviews, written specifically for inclusion in a newspaper, blog, or magazine.

Cover design and book layout by Priscilla T Graham

In the making of this book, every attempt has been made to verify names, facts, and figures.

Photos from the Graham Collection, Informer News Paper, Red Book, Mease Collection, Kautz Family YMCA Archives, and Public Domain

Written by Priscilla T Graham

priscillatgraham.com

Priscilla Graham Photography & Publishing

Dedicated to Martha. African American History is American History.

Content

Timeline	5
History	6
YMCA Colored Work Department	9
Booker T Washington	13
Julius Rosenwald	14
History of the Y Logo	17
Houston, Texas	19
World War I	25
Women of the YMCA Colored Work Department	31
Dr. Benjamin Jesse Covington	35
World War I Emergency Training Centers	36
Texas Jim Crow Laws	39
The Houston Munity and Riot 1917	40
NAACP	42
Colored Branch 1918-1931	44
Colored Branch 1932-1941	52

TIMELINE

1853-First Colored YMCA organized in Washington, DC

1866-Second Colored YMCA organized in Charleston, South Carolina

1867- Third Colored YMCA organized in New York City, New York

1867-EVC Eato, New York City President, first Colored delegate to attend an International YMCA Convention in Montreal

1869-First Colored Student Association organized at Howard University

1876-General George D. Johnson, ex-confederate soldier, appointed as the first Secretary of the Colored Association at the Toronto Convention

1879-Henry Edwards Brown appointed as the second traveling Secretary of the International Committee

1888-William A. Hunton first YMCA fulltime Colored Secretary

1890-William A. Hunton succeed Brown as International Secretary

1891- The end of White Supervision and the beginning of Colored Leadership in the YMCA

1912-First Student Conference held at King's Mountain, North Carolina for the Colored Men's Department of the YMCA

1913-Hampton Institute dedicated the first building for a student association

History

London, England

The Young Men's Christian Association was founded by George Williams in London, England on June 6, 1844. Twenty-two-year-old Williams, a draper's shop assistant, and 11 friends organized the organization's first Young Men's Christian Association Bible study and prayer for young men seeking escape from the dangers of life on the streets.

For its time, The Y was unique. It was founded to meet the social need of the community in response to unhealthy social conditions arising in the big cities at the end of the Industrial Revolution. The organization's openness to its members crossed all English social class lines.

Boston, United States

Inspired by the English stories retired Boston sea captain thirty-year-old Thomas Valentine Sullivan, a marine missionary, formed the first United States Young Men's Christian Association (YMCA) at the Old South Church in Boston to create a safe *home away from home* for sailors and merchants to escape the temptations of the large city on December 29, 1851. The Sullivan YMCA opened in 1853. The Y offered many features and activities for its 1,500 members including a reading room, library, popular lecture series, social gatherings, excursions, a gym, employment department, boarding house, and bible classes.

Washington, District of Columbia

Anthony Bowen, prominent religious leader, educator, council member of the District's Seventh Ward, the first African American clerk at the US Patent Office, and founder and president of the world's first African American YMCA, was well-known for his service and leadership in establishing churches, religious instruction, and education for freedmen in the District of Columbia.

In 1853, Anthony Bowen founded the first Colored YMCA in the world, the 12th Street Y.

Bowen was born into slavery in Prince George's County, Maryland in 1809. After completing his daily work, Bowen moonlighted as a painter and bricklayer in order to earn enough money to purchase his freedom for $425 in 1830. After purchasing his wife's freedom, he moved his family to Washington, District of Columbia.

Anthony Bowen was committed to the social, educational, and religious advancement of Colored people. He was respected in both white and black communities.

The 12th Street Colored YMCA was an Independent YMCA until 1905 when it became a branch of the YMCA of the City of Washington. As an Independent YMCA, activities were restricted to meetings in rented spaces, donated rooms, and members' living rooms. The Colored YMCA was the first non-church African American institution in the United States. William Hunton became the first YMCA fulltime Colored secretary in 1888. The first YMCA conference for Colored secretaries was held in 1900. By 1896, there were sixty active Colored Ys. Forty-one of those 60 Colored YMCAs were Ys at colleges. The first college Colored YMCA was organized at Howard University, Washington, DC in 1869. There were 160 Colored YMCAs with 28,000 members by 1924.

John Raleigh Mott

John Raleigh Mott was born the third child among four children born to Elmira Dodge and John Mott on May 25, 1865 in Livingston Manor, New York. The couple and their four children moved to Postville, Iowa where Mott's father became a lumber merchant and was elected the town's first mayor.

At sixteen, Mott enrolled at Upper Iowa University, a small Methodist preparatory school and college in Fayette. He was an enthusiastic student of history and literature there and a prizewinner in debating and oratory, but transferred to Cornell University in 1885.

On January 14, 1886, after hearing J. Kynaston Studd lecture, Mott's ideas about the future changed. The following three sentences in Studd's speech *Seekest thou great things for thyself? Seek them not. Seek ye first the Kingdom of God* galvanized his lifelong service of presenting Christ to students.

In 1886, Mott represented Cornell University's YMCA at the First International, Interdenominational Student Christian Conference. 251 men from eighty-nine colleges and universities attended the Conference; however, only one hundred including Mott vowed to work in foreign missions. As a result, the Student Volunteer Movement for Foreign Missions was organized two years later. While at Cornell, Mott was president of the University's YMCA and a member of Phi Beta Kappa. He increased the membership and raised money for a new YMCA building. In 1885, Mott and Karl Fries organized the World's Student Christian Federation. As the General Secretary, he traveled the world organizing national student movements in India, China, Japan, Australia, New Zealand, Europe, and North East.

Mott graduated from Cornell University in 1888 with a Bachelor's Degree in Philosophy and History. He assumed the position as National Secretary of The Intercollegiate YMCA of the United States and Canada in September 1888. Mott married Leila Ada White of Wooster, Ohio, on November 26, 1891. The couple had four children, John, Irene, Fredrick, and Eleanor.

By 1910, he was the Chairman of the Student Volunteer Movement for Foreign Missions, presiding officer of the World Missionary Conference in Edinburgh, Scotland, and Chairman of the International Missionary Council. Throughout his travels from 1912-13, Mott held twenty-one regional missionary conferences in India, China, Japan, and Korea.

Mott was the General Secretary of the International Committee YMCA for thirteen years, 1915 through 1928 and President of the YMCA's World Committee 1926 through 1928. He volunteered YMCA services to President Woodrow Wilson to run military canteens in the United States and France during

World War I. As a result, Mott became General Secretary of the National War Work Council and received the Distinguished Service Medal. Mott lead the relief work efforts in many countries to provide for prisoners of war and served as a member of the Mexican Commission in 1916 and member of the Special Delegation to Russia in 1917.

During his lifetime, John Raleigh Mott wrote sixteen books, navigated the Atlantic over one hundred times and the Pacific fourteen times, delivered thousands of speeches; and chaired countless conferences. He received honorary awards and decorations from China, Czechoslovakia, Finland, France, Greece, Hungary, Italy, Japan, Jerusalem, Poland, Portugal, Siam, Sweden, and the United States. Mott also received six honorary degrees from the universities of Brown, Edinburgh, Princeton, Toronto, Yale, Upper Iowa; and an honorary degree from the Russian Orthodox Church of Paris (The Nobel Foundation, 1946). In 1946, Mott and Emily Greene Balch were co-recipients of the Nobel Peace Prize. After Leila's death in 1952, he married Agnes Peters of Washington, District of Columbia in 1953.

Mott died at his home in Orlando, Florida on January 31, 1955. He was eighty-nine years old.

YMCA Colored Work Department

George D. Johnston

At the YMCA Convention in Toronto, Canada in 1876, Joseph Hardie, a white southerner, urged delegates to raise $500 to support the hiring of a *suitable man* to organize Colored YMCAs in the South. The delegates pledged $700 within minutes including a $100 pledge from founder George Williams.

As a result, George D. Johnston, a former Confederate general, was hired as a traveling secretary for Colored Association Work in the South.

Henry Edwards Brown

Henry Edwards Brown, a northerner and an abolitionist, succeeded Johnston as traveling secretary for Colored Association work in 1879. Brown was the first college president of Talladega College founded by freedmen, William Savery and Thomas Tarrant, on November 20, 1865.

The Founders, William Savery and Thomas Tarrant, asked General Wager Swayne of the Freedmen´s Bureau for help to purchase the nearby Baptist Academy that was about to be sold under mortgage default. The building was built by slaves including Savery and Tarrant in 1852-53 for white students.

General Swayne answered their plea by persuading the American Missionary Association to purchase the building and 20 acres of land for $23,000. The school was renamed the Swayne School in honor of the general and opened its doors with 140 students in November 1867. Brown was appointed the state's first private, liberal arts college dedicated to servicing the educational needs of Colored people, first president in 1869. The Judge of Probate of Talladega County issued the Swayne School a charter as Talladega College in 1869. Brown was the school's president until 1879.

William Alphaeus Hunton, Sr.

William Alphaeus Hunton was born to Stanton Hunton and Mary Ann Conyer, in Chatham, Ontario on October 31, 1863. Stanton, a brick mason, purchased his freedom in 1843 and moved to Canada. Hunton's mother died when he was four years old. His father raised Hunton and his eight brothers and sisters. Hunton graduated from Wilberforce Institute in 1884. After graduating from the Institute, he taught school in Dresden, Ontario until joining the Department of Indian Affairs in Ottawa as a probationary clerk in May 1885.

Hunton joined the local YMCA in Ottawa. He sang in the choir and became a member of the Sunday School staff resulting in him being appointed as the chairman of the Boys' Department. Hunton later resigned from the Department of Indian Affairs and moved to the United States. William Alphaeus Hunton became the first YMCA full-time Colored Secretary on January 20, 1888. At the Norfolk, Virginia Colored YMCA, he organized debating societies, educational classes, athletic work, choral club, a bible study group, and library. In 1891, Hunton wrote a pamphlet, First Steps, describing his vision for the YMCA on race relations.

During the Spanish American War, Hunton worked with soldiers in Army camps. He also established Colored Student YMCA's throughout the South. Hunton was the first National Colored Secretary hired by the International Committee of the YMCA to head the newly established Colored Men's Department. He traveled throughout the United States helping communities raise money to meet Julius Rosenwald's Challenge. Hunton helped recruit and train staff and volunteers to lead the associations.

In 1905, Hunton meet with several Negro leaders in Houston, Texas including T.M. Fairchild, L.H. Spivey and E.O. Smith to discuss establishing a Houston YMCA for Negroes; however, a Houston YMCA for Negroes was not established until after World War I. Hunton, Moorland, and Haynes launched the YMCA Training School for Colored Secretaries in 1907.

Jesse Edward Moorland

Jesse Edward Moorland, an only child, was born to William Edward and Nancy Jane Moorland on September 10, 1863 in Coldwater, Ohio. Moorland grandparents raised him after the death of his mother. He married Lucy Corbin in 1886. They both taught school in Urbana, Ohio and later moved to Washington, DC to continue their education. Moorland graduated from Howard University with a degree in Theology in 1891. He also became an ordained minister in the Congregational Church and was hired as the first General Secretary of the Colored YMCA in Washington. In 1893, he resigned from the YMCA and moved to Nashville, Tennessee to pastor Howard Chapel. Moorland later moved again in 1896 to Cleveland, Ohio to pastor Mount Zion Congregational Church. In 1898, Moorland was hired by the International Committee to assist William A. Hunton, Sr.

He became the administrator and fundraiser for the Colored YMCA Men's Department raising over $2 million to build 29 new YMCA facilities in large cities across the United States. Hunton, Moorland, and Haynes launched the YMCA Training School for Colored Secretaries in 1907. Carter G. Woodson and Moorland founded the Association for the Study of Negro Life and History in 1915. After Hunton's death, Moorland was appointed the Senior Secretary of the Colored Work Department in 1916.

Channing Heggie Tobias

Channing Heggie Tobias was born on February 1, 1882 in Augusta, Georgia to Fair J. and Clara Belle Robinson. His mother, a domestic worker, and father, a coachman, both lived in their employers' homes. As a result, Tobias was raised by his mother's friend. It is unclear why he used the name Tobias rather than Robinson.

Tobias was called to preach at the early age of 12. In 1900, he was ordained as a minister of the Colored Methodist Episcopal Church.

Tobias graduated from Paine College in 1902 with a Bachelor of Arts. In

1905, he graduated from Drew Theological Seminary, Madison, New Jersey with a Bachelor of Divinity. Three years later, Tobias received a Doctor of Divinity from the University of Pennsylvania located in Philadelphia, Pennsylvania.

Channing Heggie Tobias married Mary C. Pritchard in 1908. They had two children. For a short time after leaving Pennsylvania, Tobias served as a professor of Biblical Literature at Paine College. In 1924, he received an honorary Doctor of Divinity from Gammon Theological Seminary, Atlanta, Georgia.

Tobias joined the YMCA in 1905 serving as the Student Secretary for the International Committee. He later became the Secretary of the National Council in Washington, DC in 1911. Tobias served as the National Council Secretary for twelve years before becoming the Senior Secretary of the Colored Division of the National Council in 1923. The council's headquarters was located in New York City, New York.

In 1926, Tobias was a delegate and speaker at the 1926 World Conference in Finland. This was his crowning public achievement in interracial affairs to promote interracial cooperation and redress racial grievances. Tobias criticized the American Y for permitting racial discrimination within its own ranks and for ignoring *flagrant violations* of the Fourteenth and Fifteenth Amendments in the wider society. In 1936, Tobias noted that the United States and South Africa were almost the only countries in the world that maintained segregated Ys. Although resolutions on racial justice were passed, Tobias dismissed them as mere *expressions of conviction and hope*, because the resolutions supported no requirements for action. Tobias' persistence on this matter was a tribute to his courage and the Y's continuing willingness to retain a foreign representative who was such an outspoken critic. Tobias believed that until true equality was achieved, Colored Ys must hold on to separate associations that they administered, rather than accept subordinate status in white controlled groups. For this reason, Tobias accepted his separate, racially defined department within the Y and repeatedly emphasized the importance of the network of Colored controlled Ys across the country. Tobias told one critic that *The Y is our source of refuge*.

However, the depression eroded The Colored Y's funding resulting in services for Negroes being cut drastically. By 1934, the number of Colored YMCAs across the country fell from 179 to 50. In 1946, segregation as a national policy ended when the National Council passed a resolution to eliminate all discrimination within local YMCA associations across the country resulting in the Colored Work Department was being dissolved and abolishment of racial designations in all its publications.

President Franklin Roosevelt appointed Tobias to the National Advisory Committee on Selective Service during World War II. He was appointed by President Harry Truman in 1946 to the Civil Rights Committee.

In 1946, Tobias also became the first Colored Director of the Phelps-Stokes Fund, a foundation devoted to the improvement of educational opportunities for Negro children.

YMCA Colored Work Department Staff 1925

Front row, left to right
Robert P. Hamlin, Channing H. Tobias, and Robert DeFrantz

Back row, left to right
L.K. McMillian, William Curtis Craver, John H. McGrew, Ralph W. Bullock, and Frank T. Wilson

In 1948, Tobias' wife, Mary, died and he received the NAACP's coveted Spingarn Medal for distinguished work in race relations. He married Eva Arnold in 1951.

Tobias was an Alternate Representative of the United States for the Sixth Assembly to the United Nations in Paris, France on December 1, 1951. He served on the NAACP's board and as chairman in 1953.

Tobias died on November 5, 1961.

Booker T Washington

On April 5, 1856, Booker Taliaferro Washington was born into slavery on a plantation in Franklin County, Virginia near Hale's Ford. His mother's name was Jane and his father was an unknown white man. Jane was the slave of James Burroughs.

The Civil War ended when Washington was nine years old. Washington recalls the day in his 1901 book Up from Slavery to the White House: *As the great day drew nearer, there was more singing in the slave quarters than usual. It was bolder, had more ring, and lasted later into the night. Most of the verses of the plantation songs had some reference to freedom... Some man who seemed to be a stranger (a United States officer, I presume) made a little speech and then read a rather long paper, the Emancipation Proclamation, I think. After the reading, we were told that we were all free, and could go when and where we pleased. My mother, who was standing by my side, leaned over and kissed her children, while tears of joy ran down her cheeks. She explained to us what it all meant, that this was the day for which she had been so long praying, but fearing that she would never live to see."* Jane immediately moved her family to West Virginia to join her husband Washington Ferguson.

When Washington was ten years old, he worked as a houseboy for a white family. He also worked in a salt furnace and coal mines to earn money to further his education. Washington attended and worked his way through Hampton Institute in 1862 at the age of 16. He later attended Wayland Seminary, Washington, DC for six months. After graduating, Washington returned to Hampton Institute and became a teacher.

Former Union Brevet Brigadier General Sam Chapman Armstrong, Hampton Institute's President, recommend the 25-year-old Washington to head Tuskegee Institute in 1881. Washington modeled Tuskegee Institute after Armstrong's philosophy at Hampton Institute.

Washington was married to Fannie N. Smith, Olivia A. Davidson, and Margaret James Murray. He fathered three children, Portia M. Washington, Booker T. Washington Jr., and Ernest Davidson Washington. Washington credits his three wives for their contributions to the success of Tuskegee Institute. The success of Tuskegee Institute won Washington support amongst Colored leaders and northern white philanthropists especially Julius Rosenwald.

In 1895, during his Atlanta Compromise address at the Cotton States Exposition, Washington struck the keynotes of racial accommodationism: *Cast down your buckets where you are. In all things that are purely social, we can be as separate as the fingers, yet one as the hand in all things essential to mutual progress.* Washington was an educator, author, orator, and adviser to United States Presidents Theodore Roosevelt and William Howard Taft.

Julius Rosenwald

Julius Rosenwald was born on August 12, 1862 a few blocks from President Abraham Lincoln's residence in Springfield, Illinois to Samuel Rosenwald and Augusta Hammerslough, a Jewish immigrant couple from Germany.

When Rosenwald was 16 years old, he became an apprentice to learn the clothing trades from his uncles in New York. Rosenwald and his younger brother, Morris, started a clothing manufacturing company; however, the recession of 1885 caused the business to fail.

The brothers did not give up. They moved their manufacturing facility closer to Chicago's rural population and implemented a clothing manufacturing system according to standardized sizes from data collected during the Civil War. The Rosenwald brothers enlisted the help of their cousin, Julius Weil, and together they founded Rosenwald and Weil Clothiers. In 1883, Rosenwald and Weil Clothiers became a principal supplier of men's clothing for the Sears, Roebuck and Company.

Julius Rosenwald and Chicago businessman Aaron Nusbaum purchased half of the company in August 1895 for $75,000. The company reincorporated in Chicago and Nusbaum was bought out in 1903 for $1.3 million.

In 1906, Rosenwald's friend Paul J. Sachs introduced him to William H. Baldwin and Booker T. Washington, two prominent educators and advocates of African American education.

Rosenwald became the president and chief operating officer of the world's largest retailer, Sears, Roebuck and Company in 1909.

Rosenwald Challenge Grant
In 1910, Jesse Moorland convinced Rosenwald, to contribute a

COLORED YMCAS

Treat people fairly and honestly and generously and their response will be fair and honest and generous.

Location	Year
Washington, District of Columbia	
12th Street	1912
Philadelphia, Pennsylvania	
Christian Street	1912
Chicago, Illinois	
Wabash Avenue	1913
Indianapolis, Indiana	
Senate Avenue	1913
Kansas City, Missouri	
Paseo Department	1914
Cincinnati, Ohio	
9th Street	1916
Brooklyn, New York	
Carlton Avenue	1917
Baltimore, Maryland	
Druid Hill Avenue	1918
St. Louis, Missouri	
Pine Street	1919
Columbus, Ohio	
Spring Street	1918
New York City, New York	
135th Street	1919
Atlanta, Georgia	
Butler Street	1920
Pittsburg, Pennsylvania	
Centre Avenue	1923
Denver, Colorado	
Glenarm Branch	1924
Detroit, Michigan	
St. Antoine	1925
Los Angeles, California	
28th Street	1926
Buffalo, New York	
Michigan Avenue	1928
Dayton, Ohio	
5th Street	1928
Montclair, New Jersey	
Washington Street	1928
Evanston	1929
Toledo, Ohio	
Indiana Avenue	1930
Dallas, Texas	
Moorland	1930
Youngstown, Ohio	
West Federal Street	1931
Orange, New Jersey	
Oakwood Avenue	1932
Harrisburg, Pennsylvania	
Forster Street	1933
New York	1933

matching grant of $25,000 to any city willing to raise at least $75,000 over a five-year period for the construction of a new Colored Young Men's Christian Association branch. However, Rosenwald had one condition that he would give the money only after $50,000 was raised locally and actually extended for land and the building. The community rallied around this cause. For instance, twenty-five percent, 10,000, of Chicago Colored population contributed over $67,000 to the Wabash Y fund.

Rosenwald contributed a total of $637,000 towards the cost of building twenty-six Colored YMCAs throughout the country in 25 cities from 1911 to 1933. The local Colored population contributed $472, 319, Whites and other sources contributed $4,490,893 toward the construction of these facilities. The construction total cost was $5,815,969. There were four Colored YMCAs built in New York City.

The Rosenwald Fund
Booker T. Washington asked Rosenwald to serve on Tuskegee Institute's Board of Directors in 1912. Rosenwald created an $50,000 endowment for the institute in order to ensure that Washington was able to devote his time and efforts to running the school rather than fundraising. He gave Tuskegee $25,000 for a teacher-training program.

With the encouragement from Booker T. Washington to address the poor state of Negro education in the United States, Rosenwald allowed Washington to use a portion of the $25,000 for a pilot program to build six small schools in rural Alabama in 1913 and 1914. The schools were overseen by Tuskegee Institute. Rosenwald later donated $30,000 to build 100 rural school and an additional donation to build 200 schools.

In 1917, he established the Julius Rosenwald Fund for the well-being of mankind. The Rosenwald Fund was designed to use all of its funds for philanthropic purposes as a self-expiring fund to go out of existence following Rosenwald's death.

The Rosenwald Fund's matching school grants varied from $500 to $2,100 depending on the number of teachers to be employed. Communities were required to contribute cash and in-kind donations of material and labor to match the grant. The Rosenwald Fund school building program contributed over $4 million in matching funds to help build more than 5,000 *Rosenwald Schools* and 4,000 libraries employing over 14,000 teachers throughout the South for poor rural colored children.

Rosenwald helped the United States Department of Agriculture

COLORED SCHOOLS

The horrors that are due to race prejudice come home to the Jew more forcefully than to others of the white race, on account of the centuries of persecution which they have suffered and still suffer.

Houston, Texas

Belo School	1921-22	
One Teacher Type	$1,746.00	
Cedar Creek School	1925-26	
Two Teacher Type	$3,275.00	
Cooper School	1925-26	
One Teacher Type	$2,000.00	
Creek School	1925-26	
Two Teacher Type	$3,100.00	
Crockett Dist. School	1924-25	
Six Teacher Type	$30,000.00	
Daily School	1922-23	
Two Teacher Type	$1,850.00	
Fodice School	1922-23	
Four Teacher Type	$4,100.00	
Friendship School	1928-29	
Three Teacher Type	$3,725.00	
Gudeblye School, CTS	1923-24	
Four Teacher Type	$4,400.00	
Holly School	1926-27	
Two Teacher Type	$3,200.00	
Mount Zion School	1920-21	
One Teacher Type	$2,250.00	
New Salem School	1921-22	
One Teacher Type	$1,800.00	
Pleasant Grove School	1925-26	
Three Teacher Type	$4,100.00	
Porter Springs School	1921-22	
One Teacher Type	$1,750.00	
Post Oak School	1929-30	
Four Teacher Type	$3,500.00	
Ratcliff School	1920-21	
One Teacher Type	$2,200.00	
Rock Hill School	1921-22	
One Teacher Type	$2,000.00	
Shiloh School	1921-22	
One Teacher Type	$1,750.00	
Teacher's Home at Gudeblye School, County Training School	1926-27	
Home Type	$2,500.00	

launch a very important rural program by contributing $1,000 grants to the first 100 counties in the United States to hire County Extension Agents.

Rosenwald established the Museum of Science and Industry in Chicago in 1926. He contributed $5 million to create a museum in the style of Munich, Germany's Deutsche Museum he and his family visited in 1911. Rosenwald served as the museum's president from 1927-1932.

In addition, Rosenwald invested heavily in the University of Chicago and he also founded public school dental infirmaries. In 1928, the Fund donated over $1 million dollars to Howard, Fisk, Atlanta, and Dillard Universities. The Fund also provided financial assistance to medical institutions training doctor and nurses. Provident Hospital in Chicago, Flint-Goodridge Hospital in New Orleans, and Andrew Memorial Hospital in Alabama. Fellowship and scholarships were given to exceptional Colored students in their fields of study.

Throughout his lifetime, Rosenwald and the Rosenwald Fund invested over $70 million in public schools, colleges and universities, museums, Jewish charities, and African American institutions.

Julius Rosenwald died on January 6, 1932 at his Ravinia, Highland Park, Illinois home. However, The Rosenwald Fund was not completely spent until 1948.

COLORED SCHOOLS

Fort Bend, Texas

Bassett Farm School	1928-29	
Two Teacher Type	$3,100.00	
Crab School	1924-25	
Two Teacher Type	$3,300.00	
Missouri City School	1920-21	
Two Teacher Type	$3,500.00	
Mount Pleasant School	1922-23	
Two Teacher Type	$2,750.00	
Shop at Powell School	1930-31	
Shop Type	$2,600.00	
Shop Sugarland School	1928-29	
Shop Type	$1,200.00	
Sugarland School	1927-28	
Two Teacher Type	$6,925.00	
Shop and Library		
Teacher's Home CTS	1922-23	
Home Type	$2,400.00	
Thompson School	1922-23	
One Teacher Type	$2,350.00	

Montgomery County, Texas

Montgomery School	1929-30	
Six Teacher Type	$10,000.00	
Willis School	1929-30	
Six Teacher Type	$7,500.00	

History of the Y Logo

 In 1881, the Y logo featuring a reference to John 17:21: *"That they may all be one ... as We are one"* and highlighting the Y values was approved by the Ninth Conference in London.

 The red triangle with equal sides representing man's essential unity, body, mind, and spirit was proposed as the Y symbol by Dr. Luther Halsey Gulick, Jr., Director of the Physical Education Department of the YMCA Training School, in 1891.

 The decision to add the triangle to the old World Alliance Insignia was authorized by the United States and Canadian Ys at the 1895 Annual Convention.

 In 1896, a second ring representing friendship and love without end among individuals was added to the logo. This logo is the Y's official emblem.

 From 1897 to 1967, the Y's everyday logo was the red triangle.

 The Y triangle and bent bar logo was created and trademarked in 1967.

In 2010, the Y created a logo to reflect the vibrancy and diversity of the communities it serves. Bold, active, and welcoming colors to reflect the Y's true identity as a caring, people oriented organization devoted to the cause of strengthening the community and social progress.

FOR YOUTH DEVELOPMENT
FOR HEALTHY LIVING
FOR SOCIAL RESPONSIBILITY

FOR YOUTH DEVELOPMENT
FOR HEALTHY LIVING
FOR SOCIAL RESPONSIBILITY

FOR YOUTH DEVELOPMENT
FOR HEALTHY LIVING
FOR SOCIAL RESPONSIBILITY

FOR YOUTH DEVELOPMENT
FOR HEALTHY LIVING
FOR SOCIAL RESPONSIBILITY

FOR YOUTH DEVELOPMENT
FOR HEALTHY LIVING
FOR SOCIAL RESPONSIBILITY

Houston, Texas

The Houston Young Men's Christian Association was founded in 1885 by a group of businessmen. They met in the old Pilot Opera House on Franklin Street to establish the organization, Houston Young Men's Christian Association. A permanent organization was adopted on February 7, 1886. The board of the newly organized organization met on January 21, 1886 at the Cotton Exchange to appoint a committee to find an appropriate facility for the new Y. The Committee on Membership reported that the $2,000 needed to launch the organization had been collected. The first YMCA was located in rented quarters on the second and third floors of the Brown Building at 102 Main Street at Texas Avenue. The building was owned by Mrs. A.B. Brown.

Cotton Exchange

The Houston Young Men's Christian Association was incorporated on October 8, 1889 and moved to the Smith Building at 1011 Texas Avenue after a fire in the Brown Building in 1894. The YMCA later acquired property at 918 Fannin and McKinney and moved into a small cottage in March 1902. The organization added a wood frame gym to the building.

The Y remained at 918 Fannin Street until 1941, when a new, larger building was erected at 1600 Louisiana Street and the facility was turned over to the USO to support soldiers serving in World War II.

The Houston YMCA launched a building campaign in May 1906 and broke ground on a new facility in April 1907. The cornerstone for the new magnificent 5 story structure was laid on October 19, 1907. The dedication ceremony took place on June 1, 1908. The fine building featured a lobby with two fireplaces and a marble staircase, indoor pool *plunge bath*, 4-lane bowling alley, two gyms, barbershop, handball court, boys' department, assembly hall, 11 classrooms, 91 resident rooms, locker rooms, health club, and a large game room. Instantly, the new YMCA became a magnet for serving thousands of Houstonians.

Gra Y Club members and sponsor en route to Camp Mayes at Spring, Texas

South Texas College of Law

In 1919, the Houston YMCA opened the first community YMCA in the Houston Heights. Shortly after, the YMCA Newsboys Club was organized to serve Houston's underprivileged boys.

The Houston YMCA provided many educational classes through its education department. In 1920, the YMCA Education Department was renamed the Houston School of Technology. Law classes were offered after the work day to give the working man an opportunity to attend in 1922 under the direction of A. L. Turner. As a result, the YMCA's South Texas College of Law was founded in 1923. College offices and classrooms were housed in three rooms on the third floor of the YMCA building at the corner of Fannin and McKinney streets. In 1924, the Law School received a standard rating and graduating students received Legum Baccalaureus, LLB, Bachelor of Law. The college received its accreditation in 1928. In 1967, the South Texas College of Law became an independent, nonprofit corporation. The campus is located at 1303 San Jacinto Street, Houston, Texas.

Ross S. Sterling Mansion

Architect Alfred C. Finn of Houston drew the plans for this scaled-down replica of the American White House for oil executive Ross S. Sterling (1875-1949). Completed in 1927 on the residential "Gold Coast" stretching from La Porte to Morgan's Point, it stood as a landmark on the Houston Ship Channel. By night its roof deck commanded a view of the lighted industrial plants in this region.

Layers of stone, concrete, air space, and plastered lath form the thick exterior walls. Deeply sunken foundations and huge beams running the length of the structure give it hurricane resistance.

With 21,000 square feet of floor space, this was known as the largest private residence in Texas at the time it was built. It has seven fireplaces, 15 baths, 34 rooms - including a dining room seating 300 guests. Silver and gold inlaid sconces, fine cared woods, and Tiffany chandeliers form some of the adornments. There were elaborate facilities for recreation and for efficient housekeeping. Sterling and his wife Maude Abbie (Gage) had several children.

Ross Sterling was governor of Texas 1931-1933. In 1946 he donated his mansion to a civic club and it was used as a juvenile home until 1961. **Marker** 10782 **Text:**

Camp Ross Sterling, Jr.

In 1910, Houston YMCA began Summer Camp programming on the Bolivar Peninsula. Former Governor of Texas Ross Sterling, founder of Humble Oil, donated the first camp owned by the Houston YMCA in memory of his son, Ross Sterling, Jr. in 1924. The 10-acre camp was located on Cedar Point off Trinity Bay near Baytown, Texas. The camp offered Gulf Coast boys a nurturing and structured environment to help them develop into disciplined young men.

Sam Houston owned the property prior to Sterling. This is where he built his summer cabin the Raven Moor. Camp Ross Sterling, Jr. was destroyed in 1961 by Hurricane Carla.

Trinity Bay
Pier leading to Trinity Bay

1600 Louisiana Street
Houston, Texas 77002

Downtown YMCA 10 story building designed by Kenneth Franzheim built in 1941

Young Men's Christian Association of Greater Houston

The Young Men's Christian Association of Greater Houston has grown over the years in parallel with the city's growth and expansion. Today, the organization's 40 YMCA family centers are located throughout Houston and neighboring counties.

808 Pease Street
Houston, Texas 77002

Tellepsen Family Downtown YMCA 115,000 square foot facility. Building designed by Kirksey and built in 2010

World War I

During World War I, the United States government mobilized the entire nation including all Colored citizens. However, Colored soldiers were not allowed to serve in the Marines and could only serve in a limited and menial capacity in the Navy and Coast Guard. Over one million Colored men between the ages of 21 and 31 registered for the draft and 370,000 were inducted into the United States Army all Colored units. Initially, before the War Department created the 92nd and 93rd Combat Divisions, there were only four all Colored regiments-the 9th and 10th Cavalry and the 24th and 25th Infantry. These units were not used in overseas combat. They were dispersed throughout the United States and assigned to service units.

The 369th Infantry, *Harlem Hellfighters*, of the 93rd Colored Combat Division were the first Colored soldiers to set foot on French soil. They were followed by the 370th Infantry, *The Black Devils*, on July 6, 1918. However, neither unit were not allowed to fight with the American Expeditionary Forces. General John Pershing, Commander of the American Expeditionary Forces, Colored soldiers from the 92nd and 93rd Combat Divisions fought with the French Expeditionary Forces. The trench warfare in Europe was brutal. The trenches were continuously under attack, bloody, and muddy. To help soldiers cope with the

wounds and harsh reality of war, the Young Men's Christian Association under the leadership of John Raleigh Mott, General Secretary of the International Committee YMCA, volunteered its services to President Woodrow Wilson to run military canteens in the United States and France. The Colored Work Department was assigned the responsibility for Colored soldiers under the War Work Council.

The YMCA was one of seven volunteer organizations that made up the United War Work Campaign designed to raise $170,500,000 to help boost soldiers' morale and provide them with recreational activities. These private organizations, the National War Council of the YMCA, the War Work Council of the YWCA, the War Camp Community Service, Red Cross, American Library Association, the National Catholic War Council-Knights of Columbus, Jewish Welfare Board, and Salvation Army, provided entertainment, counseling, religious services, athletic programs, nursing, and much more for soldiers. Under Mott's leadership, the YMCA raised over $235 million for relief work.

Through the National War Work Council Young Men's Christian Associations of the United States, Mott hired 25,926 Y workers to serve and provide welfare services for troops in the United States and France. There were twenty-three Colored women Y Secretaries and nineteen canteen workers among the 5,145 Y women workers hired. These Y workers operated 1,500 canteens and set up 4,000 Y huts for recreation and religious services for soldiers and sailors overseas. Three hundred Colored YMCA Secretaries including three educational specialists, and nineteen female canteen workers were assigned to the Colored Work Department under the leadership of Dr. J.E. Moorland, Senior Secretary of the Negro Men's Department of the International Committee, to serve Colored soldiers in fifty-five camps, seven training schools, and three forts. Sixty served overseas and in East Africa. Fourteen additional Secretaries served with Student Army Training Corps units in Colored colleges. Three hundred and seventy-four Colored secretaries served during World War I. They were housed in barracks, mess halls, tents, and twenty-five E type and National Guard buildings.

Whenever the military permitted, temporary huts were erected near the front lines in combat zones. These secretaries often went into the most advanced trenches with soldiers doing their best to keep up the soldiers' spirits and fighting morale. They also served the troops tobacco, coffee, chocolate, and provided other canteen services.

Big YMCA tent for Colored soldiers near the front in France. The YMCA provided Colored soldiers the same service as white soldiers.

Dr. James E. Moorland
Senior Secretary of Colored Men's Department International YMCA

Under Dr. Jesse E. Moorland's leadership, an estimated two million soldiers attended these various centers for Colored troops each month; two hundred lectures with an average of eighty soldiers attending monthly; ten thousand Scriptures were in circulation monthly; nine thousand personal interviews; seven thousand Christian decisions; eleven thousand war roll singers; one hundred and twenty-five thousand taking part in physical activities; five hundred motion picture exhibitions with an attendance of three hundred thousand; 1,250,000 letters written., and $110,000 worth of money orders sold (E.J. Scott. The American Negro in the World War. Chapter XXVIII).

YMCA Colored secretaries were carefully selected. Before assigning a secretary to a unit of Colored Troops, each potential secretary was thoroughly investigated and required to be a member in good standing of an evangelical church. The men were either specialist in their field or trained to become one. Secretaries were also selected based on their capacity to command the respect of the soldiers they served.
YMCA camp staff responsible for work inside the building consisted of a building secretary, religious work secretary, an educational secretary, a physical secretary, a social secretary, and a business secretary. The building secretary was the executive. The religious work secretary was in charge of all religious activities including but not limited to working with the soldiers individually, Bible Classes, and religious meetings. The educational secretary was charged with encouraging intellectual development and promoting lectures and educational classes. The physical secretary was usually in charge of all athletics and various activities for the physical welfare of the soldiers in the camp. He worked very close with the military officers. The social secretary promoted social activities, entertainments, stunts, and moving pictures. The business secretary was responsible for recording and documenting monetary transactions. Thousands of soldiers learned how to read and write. Within a short time, troops developed a love of reading good books and an appreciation of higher ideals giving them a more intellectual attitude toward life. Eleven of the nineteen Colored women canteen workers were stationed overseas-Helen Hagan, Rilda Phelps, Florence L. Thomas, Meta Evans, Ernestine Suarez, Hattie Craigwell, Lillian W. Turner, Florence C. Williams, Harriett S. Edwards, Alethea E. Rochon, and Laura G. Williamson.

Officials of the Young Men's Christian Association Department for Colored Troops. Front Row, Left to Right--William J. Faulkner, Placement; Jesse E. Moorland, Executive Secretary, Robert B. DeFrantz, Personnel. Back Row, Left to Right-Geo. L. Johnson. Religious work: Max Yergan, Overseas; Franz Gregory, Religious Work.

Group of Y Workers with Secretary Snyder and staff at YMCA No. 7, Camp Grant, Illinois

YMCA Secretaries stationed overseas…

Group of YMCA Secretaries preparing to sail overseas for France.

B. F. Seldon after returning from a trip through the trenches behind the lines in France.

In 1918, Mrs. James L. Curtis (Helen M. Noble Curtis) was the first Colored woman to sail to France as a YMCA Secretary with the American Expeditionary Forces. Kathryn Magnolia Johnson and Addie Waites Hunton followed three weeks later. The three women helped operate the largest YMCA Huts in France built for Colored Soldiers at Camp Lusitania, St. Nazaire, and Chambery serving over 150,000 soldiers. Sixteen additional Y women, Dr. N. Fairfax Brown, Mrs. Childs, Mrs. Williamson, Miss Evans, Miss Thomas, Mrs. Williams, Mrs. Craigwell, Miss Bruce, Miss Garbon, Miss Rochon, Miss Edwards, Miss Phelps, Miss Saurez, and Miss Turner, arrived in the spring of 1919. They worked in groups of twos but the first three women that arrived in the France camp were separated and disbursed alone to different camps working a minimum of 12 hours per day, 9am-9pm.

Mary Burnett Talbert, President of the National Association of Colored Women, served as YMCA Secretary and Red Cross nurse for four months with the American Expeditionary Forces during her tour of duty in Romange, France in 1919. She was the last woman to arrive for overseas work. Talbert taught classes on religion and conducted lectures to help boost the Colored soldiers' morale. *Talbert joined Mrs. Curtis at Romange. There she won the hearts of the soldiers completely. They gave her a purse of $1,000 for the Frederick Douglass Home at Anacostia, which through Mrs. Talbert's untiring efforts, has been made a national memorial for colored Americans.*

The only Colored performing artist sent to France was composer pianist Miss Helen Eugenia Hagan.

Women of the YMCA Colored Work Department

Helen M. Noble Curtis

Mrs. Helen Curtis and her soldiers Chambery, France

Helen M. Noble Curtis was born on October 10, 1874, in New Orleans, Louisiana. In May 1918, Mrs. Helen M. Noble Curtis was the first Colored woman to sail to France as a YMCA Secretary with the American Expeditionary Forces. She was a member of the Committee of Management of The Colored Women's Branch of the YWCA for many years and volunteer at Camp Upton's hostess house. Her late husband, James Logan Curtis, was Minister Resident and Consul General for the United States to Liberia. Mrs. Curtis lived in Monrovia, Liberia until her husband's death in October 1917. Throughout her many travels, Curtis also lived in France where she studied domestic art for two years and learned the language. Mrs. Curtis spoke the French language fluently. This made her a perfect YMCA Secretary candidate. As a result, Helen's appointment was very successful resulting in twenty-two women being appointed as YMCA Secretaries to the American Expeditionary Forces to serve Colored soldier overseas.

In November 1918, Curtis barely escaped deportation for fostering, in the words of army intelligence, notions of complete social recognition and other objectionable matter calculated to make trouble. Mrs. Curtis case demonstrated the hostility of the YMCA toward Colored control of Colored facilities and the caution of the United States Army about permitting educated Colored Civilians close contact with troops. Mrs. Curtis worked tirelessly to clear herself and the other Colored YMCA Secretaries of any wrong doings. Through her energy the facts were investigated, and the workers were sent back to their positions, and made a remarkable record (WEB DuBois memo to NAACP Spingarn Medal Letter, January 23, 1920).

Kathryn Magnolia Johnson

Kathryn Magnolia Johnson was born on December 15, 1878 in Darke County, Ohio to Lucinda Jane McCown and Walter Johnson. Kathryn graduated from high school in New Paris, Ohio in 1895 and taught school in Ohio and Indiana from 1898 through 1901.

Hut 5, Camp Lusitania, St. Nazaire. The largest YMCA hut in France with full staff of three secretaries. From left to right: JC Croom, Kathryn M. Johnson, FO Nichols, traveling Lecturer on Civics, and Walter Price

She attended Wilberforce University and graduated in 1902 with a Bachelor's degree and teaching certificate. Kathryn taught school from 1904 to 1905 at the State Normal School for Negroes in Elizabeth City, North Carolina. In 1906, she became the Dean of Women at Shorter College in Little Rock, Arkansas. During the Argenta Race Riot of 1906, African American women and children gathered at the college for protection from armed white men roaming the streets killing African Americans and burning their property. Johnson was one of the first members of the National Association for the Advancement of Colored People (NAACP) in 1909.

She taught at Kansas City High School in 1910. Kathryn eventually left the teaching profession and became the sales representative for the NAACP's Crisis Magazine. Within three years, she became a branch organizer establishing many NAACP branches in the South. The NAACP let Kathryn go in 1916 because she openly spoke out against the dominance of whites' leadership roles within the NAACP.

In 1918, Kathryn Magnolia Johnson and Addie Waites Hunton sail to France as Young Men's Christian Association (YMCA) Secretaries with the American Expeditionary Forces. The women helped operate the largest YMCA Huts in France built for Colored Soldiers at Camp Lusitania, St. Nazaire, and Chambery serving over 150,000 soldiers. After the war, Kathryn and Addie published their book, Two Colored Women with the American Expeditionary Forces, documenting their experiences in 1920. The book detailed the cultural climate in France toward Colored soldiers and highlights the ill treatment of the soldiers with the American Expeditionary Forces in France.

Kathryn joined Carter G. Woodson's Association for the Study of Negro Life and Literature, Chicago Campaign to spread Colored literature throughout the country in 1919. By 1928, Kathryn had traveled over 9,000 miles selling Colored authors' works published by the Association. She sold 15,000 books.

Addie D. Waites Hunton

Addie D. Waites Hunton was born on June 11, 1875 in Norfolk, Virginia to Adeline Lawton and Jesse Waites. Addie's mother died when she was very young. As a result, she was raised by her aunt in Boston, Massachusetts where Addie attended Boston Latin School. After graduating high school, Addie attended Spencerian College of Commerce. She was the first Colored woman to graduate from the college in 1889. Addie moved to Normal, Alabama to teach at the Normal Agricultural College.

In July 1893, Addie married William Alphaeus Hunton. Addie and William later moved to Atlanta, Georgia in 1899. The couple had four children; however, two died during infancy. The family moved to Brooklyn, New York in 1906. Addie served from 1906 to 1910 as the national organizer for the National Association of Colored Women. Hunton was appointed as the secretary of the Young Women's Christian Association in 1907 responsible for serving the Colored population. As the Colored YWCA Secretary, Addie traveled throughout the South and Midwest to recruit influential Colored women to join the YWCA.

In 1909, Addie and her two children, William and Eunice, moved to Europe. They lived in Switzerland and Strasbourg, Germany where she attended Kaiser Wilhelm College part-time. Addie continued to attend college at the College of the City of New York and work for the YWCA when they returned to the United States in 1910. Eventually, the family moved to Saranac Lake, New York until 1916 after William's death from tuberculosis.

During World War I, Kathryn Magnolia Johnson and Addie D. Waites Hunton sailed to France as Young Men's Christian Association (YMCA) Secretaries with the American Expeditionary Forces. The women helped operate the largest YMCA Huts in France built for Colored Soldiers at Camp Lusitania, St. Nazaire, and Chambery serving over 150,000 soldiers. Throughout her tour in France, Addie developed many new programs to increase the quality of soldiers' lives. However, one of Addie's most gruesome war time assignments in May 1919 was overseeing Colored soldiers assigned to recover dead bodies from the battlefield of the Meuse-Argonne and rebury them.

After the war, Kathryn and Addie published their book, Two Colored Women with the American Expeditionary Forces documenting their experiences in 1920. The book detailed the cultural climate in France toward Colored soldiers and highlights the ill treatment of the soldiers with the American Expeditionary Forces in France. In 1921, Addie advocated from Colored women voters at the National Woman's Party Convention. From 1921 through 1924, she was the National Association for the Advancement of Colored People vice president and field secretary. In 1926, Addie wrote a report condemning the United States occupation of Haiti and assisted in organizing the 1927 Pan African Congress. In 1938, she published a biography of William Alphaeus Hunton: A Pioneer Prophet of Young Men.

Addie Waites Hunton died at the age of 68 on June 21, 1943.

Mary Burnett Talbert

Mary Burnett Talbert, one of the most prominent Colored Women in the United States, was born on September 17, 1866, the third child and third daughter of Caroline Nicholls and Cornelius Burnett in Oberlin, Lorain, Ohio. When she was sixteen, Mary graduated from Oberlin High School and Oberlin College in 1886 with a Bachelors of Arts Degree.

After graduation, Mary accepted a teaching position at Bethel University in Little Rock, Arkansas. In 1887, she became the first African American Assistant Principal, the state's highest position for a Colored woman, at Little Rock High School. In 1891, Mary Burnett married William H. Talbert. The young couple moved to Buffalo, New York and had one child, Sarah May Talbert, born in May 1892.

Mary was a founding member of Buffalo, New York's first affiliate of the National Association of Colored Women, the Phyllis Wheatley Club of Colored Women, in 1899. In 1901, she spearheaded the efforts to bring nationally prominent Colored leaders such as W.E.B. DuBois and Mary Church to Buffalo, New York to speak at the Christian Culture Congress, a literary society and forum, held at Michigan Avenue Baptist Church.

In 1901, Phyllis Wheatley Club members Mrs. William H. Talbert and Mrs. John Dover along with Mrs. A.B. Wilson, president of the Central Union of the W.C.T.U. and Mr. James A. Ross lead a rally to protest the Pan American Exposition, the World's Fair held in Buffalo, for not appointing a Colored commissioner to represent the race. Ross spoke to two hundred people attending the rally about the prejudice of the Exposition officials for excluding Colored people from the Planning Commission. The Phyllis Wheatley protest resulted in a Federal appropriation of $15,000 for a special exhibit featuring cultural and economic achievements of the Negro race in America since emancipation. The exhibit was placed under the supervision of James Ross.

Mary also lectured at the Biennial Conference of the National Association of Colored Women's Clubs (NACWC) in Buffalo and was instrumental locally in the arrangements. She secretly held a meeting with W.E.B DuBois, John Hope and nearly thirty others around her dining room table for the first meeting of what would eventually become the Niagara Movement, the forerunner of the NAACP, in 1905. In 1916, she was elected the President of the National Association of Colored Women (NACW) and Vice

President of the NAACP.

During World War I, Mary Burnett Talbert served as a YMCA Secretary and Red Cross nurse for four months with the American Expeditionary Forces during her tour of duty in Romange, France in 1919. She was the last woman to arrive for overseas work. Talbert taught classes on religion and conducted lectures to help boost the Colored soldiers' morale. *Talbert joined Mrs. Curtis at Romange. There she won the hearts of the soldiers completely. They gave her a purse of $1,000 for the Frederick Douglass Home at Anacostia, which through Mrs. Talbert's untiring efforts, has been made a national memorial for colored Americans.* Thus, she was elected president for life of the Frederick Douglass Memorial and Historical Association.

After the war, the League of Nations appointed Talbert to the Women's Committee on International Relations. She returned to Europe to lecture on the importance of women's rights and race relations. She also became a dedicated advocate of the Dyer Anti–Lynching Bill introduced in 1919 by Missouri Congressman Leonidas Dyer. Talbert was the first Colored person to address the Fifth Congress of the International Council of Women in Christina, Norway in 1920. In 1921, she became chair of the NAACP's Anti–Lynching Committee. The next year, Mary B. Talbert became the first African American Women to win the NAACP's Spingarn Award, the organization's most significant honor for civil rights activity. Mary Burnett Talbert died in Buffalo, New York on October 15, 1923 at the age of 57.

Helen Eugenia Hagan

Pianist Helen Eugenia Hagan is the first Colored female to earned a music degree from Yale in 1912. She also studied in France. During world War I, she entertained Colored soldiers in France. She was the only Colored performer to do so.

Hagan is the first Colored pianist to give a recital at a concert venue in New York. She taught at Chicago's Mendelssolm Conservatory of Music and received a Master's Degree from the Teacher's College at Columbia University.

Hagan served as Dean of Music at Bishop College in Marshall, Texas.

Addie D. Waites Hunton

Kathryn Magnolia Johnson

Dr. Benjamin Jesse Covington, Jr.

Dr. Benjamin Jesse Covington, Jr. was born on December 16, 1877 in rural Falls County near Marlin, Texas. He was the son of freedmen, Benjamin and Georgiana Covington. Covington grew up on a small farm planting, chopping, and picking cotton. After graduating in 1886, he enrolled in Hearne Baptist Academy at an early age in 1892. Covington worked as a janitor and bell ringer to support himself through college. After graduation on June 3, 1892, he taught at a local school near his birthplace for a short time earning a teacher's salary of $75 per month plus $25 for private tutoring. Covington soon left because of the animosity of white community members who thought he was earning too much for a Colored teacher.

Covington moved to Houston, Texas on August 7, 1884 to work as a bookkeeper for his eldest brother's grocery store. In 1895, he enrolled at Meharry Medical College in Nashville, Tennessee. Dr. Covington graduated from medical school in 1900 and moved to Wharton, Texas to practice medicine as a doctor on a temporary permit. Dr. Covington later moved to Yoakum, Texas. He met Jennie Belle Murphy from Gonzales at a speaking engagement at Guadalupe College, Seguin, Texas. They were married on September 30, 1902. On June 18, 1903, the Covingtons moved to Houston. Their first home was located at 1904 Ennis Street. The couple's daughter, Ernestine Jesse Covington was born on May 19, 1904.

In 1910, Doctors, Rupert O. Roett, Benjamin Jesse Covington, Henry E. Lee, Charles Jackson, and French F. Stone, established Houston's first hospital for Colored Americans. Reverend Ned P. Pullum, Pastor of Friendship Baptist Church, provided funding and a facility on Andrews Street for the People's Sanitarian. The hospital opened in 1911. In 1918, the Doctors opened Union Hospital. The six-bed hospital in a remodelled house with sparse equipment was located on Howard and Nash Streets. The hospital had one surgical suite. The new Union Hospital was also located on Andrews Street. The founders eventually moved the facility into an abandoned hospital building that previously belonged to an unlicensed preacher-healer known as Mr. Jeremiah at the intersection of Genesee Street and Andrews Street in 1923. To capture the building's history, they renamed the eleven-bed hospital to the Union Jeremiah Hospital.

During World War I, the influenza epidemic of 1918-19 killed more people than the war. It was the most devastating epidemic in recorded world history killing between 20 and 40 million people within one year including 43,000 soldiers. Concerned about the impact of the epidemic on humanity, Dr. Covington trained himself in pulmonary medicine. When the United States Army Medical Corp learned of Doctor Covington's formula he developed to cure the flu, they immediately requested and secured the formula to treat soldiers for influenza resulting in thousands of lives being saved. In September and October 1918, three thousand ninety-one cases of influenza were reported at Camp Logan; however, the mortality rate was extremely low. Only eighty-four soldiers died because the Army used the vaccine developed by Doctor Covington to treat the sick soldiers.

In 1918, Doctors, Rupert O. Roett, Benjamin Jesse Covington, Henry E. Lee, Charles Jackson, and French F. Stone, appealed to wealthy oilman and philanthropist, Joseph Stephen Cullinan, for assistance to build a fifty-bed hospital. Cullinan established a fund and donated $80,000 to build the hospital. Isaiah Milligan Terrell, Houston Central College President, retired to help raise funds for the new hospital. The city of Houston donated three acres of land at Elgin and Ennis Streets to help build the new and larger hospital for the growing Colored community. Construction for the new hospital began in 1925. On June 19, 1926, the Hospital was *dedicated to the American Negro to promote self-help, to insure good citizenship and for the relief of suffering, sickness and disease among them.* The Houston Negro Hospital opened to patients on May 14, 1927 and officially opened in July 1927.

World War I Emergency Training Centers

Over 2 million American soldiers fought on the battlefields of France under the leadership of General John J. Pershing. To ensure that soldiers were well trained before going to Europe, the War Department built 32 training facilities throughout the country to rapidly train large numbers of troops.

The Young Men's Christian Association was the first religiously affiliated civilian partner approved through General Orders No. 57 issued by President Thomas Woodrow Wilson on April 26, 1917 to erect and maintain YMCA Association buildings on military reservations in both the United States and overseas for the promotion of the social, physical, intellectual, and morale welfare of enlisted men (Mott, 1917, pg. 204). Each of 32 training camps was authorized to build at least six YMCA recreational and social buildings and a maximum of fourteen buildings. The Young Men's Christian Association estimated costs to provide three hundred and sixty-two buildings, over one hundred and fifty 40 x 80 feet tents, four hundred special outfits and equipment in American training camps was $11 million. YMCA auditorium facilities were designed to provided seating for at least three thousand and furnished with a piano, motion picture machine, phonograph, office supplies, postcards, pens, ink, pencils, stationery, and reading material.

The City of Houston and its officials aggressively lobbied to be awarded one of the contacts and on June 14, 1917, Houston was awarded a $2 million government contract to build an emergency training center for a National Guard Training Center, Camp Logan. The Department of Defense chose Houston because of its moderate climate and opened ship channel. The city was later awarded a contract to build an aviation training site, Ellington Field.

Camp Logan YMCA

Camp Logan was established on July 18, 1917 in Houston, Texas as an emergency training center when the United States entered World War I on April 6, 1917. The Department of Defense chose Houston because of its moderate climate and newly opened ship channel. The 7,600-acre United States Army Camp was named in honor of General John A. Logan, Mexican War and Civil War veteran and senator from Illinois. *The Houston Mutiny and Riot of 1917*, Colored soldiers' response to Houston's Jim Crow laws, insulting racial epithets, police brutality, and fear of a white mob attack, was the camp's most publicized incident.

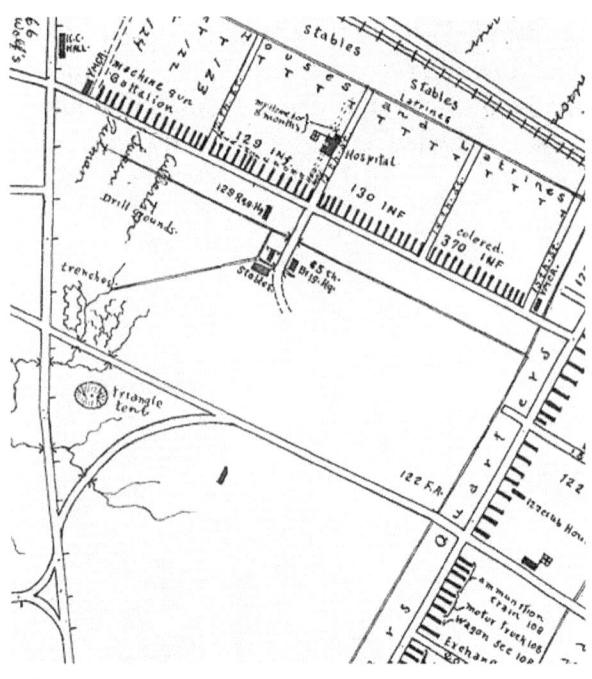

The National War Work Council, Young Men's Christian Associations of the United States initially built six YMCA facilities throughout Camp Logan. The auditorium was erected in 1918 and an officer's facility was also erected. The YMCA eventually added an additional four buildings to provide one building for every 2,500 soldiers.

The first YMCA erected in Houston to serve Colored troops was established in a tent facility near Camp Logon on the corner of 14th and 28th Streets. The opening and dedication of the new tent facility took place on October 21, 1917. The YMCA permanent structure on the corner of 14th and 28th Streets for Colored troops training in Houston was completed in December 1917. The dedication ceremony was held on December 16, 1917.

The Colored soldiers' quarters were located on the

westside of camp. The 8th Illinois Infantry received orders to report to Camp Logan for training on October 1, 1917. The unit consisted of 2,054 soldiers. The War Department activated the 8th Illinois Infantry Colored National Guard Unit and renamed them as the 370th Infantry assigned to the 93rd Division on December 1, 1917. On March 6, 1918, the soldiers left Camp Logan enroute to France. They arrived on April 22, 1918 and were sent to the front lines on July 6, 1918 under the French Army's Command. *Seventy-one African American soldiers of the 370th Infantry that trained at Camp Logan were awarded the French Croix de Guerre and 21 received the United States Army's Distinguished Service Cross for their acts of valor.*

Ellington Field YMCA

Ellington Field was the nation's first aerial bombing school and largest pilot and navigator training base in the United States. In 1917, the United States Government purchased 1,280 acres of land in southeast Houston from Dr. R.W. Knox and the Wright Company to establish the airbase. The base opened on November 27, 1917 and by the end of World War I, Ellington Field housed 20,0000 men and 250 aircrafts. The base closed after World War I and later reopened with limited use until World War II. The Ellington Field YMCA operated as a subdivision of the Camp Logan YMCA until an order approving it as a separate unit of the organization.

After the war, Mott used the money left over from the $235 million raised for wartime relief work to build new YMCAs, outreach to small towns and countries, work with returning Colored troops, and invest in YMCA trade schools and colleges. As a result, the Colored YMCA of Houston opened in February 1918 under the War Work Council, sponsored by the National YMCA. The Colored Soldiers and Sailors Branch of Houston Young Men's Christian Association (YMCA) opened on the third floor of the Lincoln Theatre under the leadership of Professor Howard Payne Carter as a center for returning World War I Colored soldiers and sailors.

Texas Jim Crow Laws 1866-1919

Twelve Jim Crow laws were passed in the State of Texas from 1866 to 1919. In 1871, Texas enacted one anti-segregation law in 1871 barring separation of the races on public carriers; however, the law was repealed in 1889.

JIM CROW LAWS

1866: Education [Constitution]
All taxes paid by blacks to go to maintaining African schools. Duty of the legislature to "encourage colored schools."

1866: Railroads [Statute]
"All railroad companies shall attach one passenger car for the special accommodation of freedmen."

1871: Barred segregation on public carriers [Statute]
Public carriers prohibited from making any distinctions in the carrying of passengers. Penalty: Misdemeanor punishable by a fine from $100 to $500, or imprisonment from 30 to 90 days, or both.

1876: Voting rights [Constitution]
Required electors to pay poll tax.

1879: Miscegenation [Statute]
Confirmed intermarriage law passed in 1858. Penalty applied equally to both parties.

1889: Railroads [Statute]
Railroad companies required to maintain separate coaches for white and colored passengers, equal in comfort. Penalty: Passengers refusing to sit where assigned were guilty of a misdemeanor, and could be fined between $5 and $20.

JIM CROW LAWS

1891: Railroads [Statute]
Separate coach laws strengthened. Separate coaches for white and Negro passengers to be equal in all points of comfort and convenience. Designed by signage posted in a conspicuous place in each compartment. Trains allowed to carry chair cars or sleeping cars for the exclusive use of either race. Law did not apply to streetcars. Penalty: Conductors who failed to enforce law faced misdemeanor charge punishable by a fine from $5 to $25. The railroad company could be fined from $100 to $1,000 for each trip. Passengers who refused to sit in designated areas faced fines from $5 to $25.

1907: Streetcars [Statute]
Required all streetcars to comply with the separate coach law passed in 1889. Penalty: Streetcar companies could be fined from $100 to $1,000 for failing to enact law. A passenger wrongfully riding in an improper coach was guilty of a misdemeanor, and faced fines from $5 to $25.

1909: Railroads [Statute]
Depot buildings required to provide separate waiting areas for the use of white and Negro passengers.

1914: Railroads [Statute]
Negro porters shall not sleep in sleeping car berths nor use bedding intended for white passengers.

1915: Miscegenation [State Code]
The penalty for intermarriage is imprisonment in the penitentiary from two to five years.

1919: Public accommodations [Statute]
Ordered that Negroes were to use separate branches of county free libraries.

The Houston Mutiny and Riot of 1917

On August 23, 1917, two white police officers, Lee Sparks and Rufe Daniels, entered the house of a respected Colored woman, Mrs. Travis, in an alleged search for a Colored fugitive accused of crap shooting. Although the policemen did not find the fugitive, they arrested the woman, striking, and forcing her out into the streets partly clad in front of her five children.

While waiting for the patrol wagon a crowd gathered around the weeping woman who had become hysterical asking why she was being arrested. Private Edwards, questioned the policemen and asked if he could take her. The police officers quickly beat Private Edwards to the ground with the butts of their guns and arrested him. Sparks stated, *I beat that nigger until he got his heart right. He was a good nigger when I got through with him.* Corporal Baltimore, member of the military police, approached and asked Sparks and Daniels about Private Edwards. Sparks opened fire and Corporal Baltimore fled with the two in pursuit. The unarmed Baltimore hide under the bed in a house in the neighborhood.

When they found Corporal Baltimore, Sparks and Daniels dragged, beat, and arrested him. When the news reached the camp, the men of the 24th Infantry were outraged to the point of revolt.

There were rumors that Corporal Baltimore had been killed. As a result, Major Snow phoned Police Headquarters to request that Corporal Baltimore be returned to Camp Logan immediately. The Major informed the soldiers about what happened and stated that Sparks would be punished; however, the soldiers were beyond their commanding officer's control.

After checking in at 8:00pm, on a hot rainy night, Acting First Sergeant Henry informed the Battalion Commander Major Kneeland S. Snow that he was riding into town with a friend, but was concerned that there may be trouble in camp. While investigating the rumor, Captain Snow caught several soldiers acquiring weapons and ammunition. He ordered Sergeant Henry and the other First Sergeants to retrieve all weapons and ammunition taken. Before they could retrieve the weapons and ammunition from the soldiers, Private Frank Johnson yelled, *Get your guns' men! The white mob is coming!* The frightened soldiers rushed the company's four supply tents to retrieve weapons and ammunition to protect themselves from the white mob and outside gunfire. The soldiers returned the outside gunfire shooting franticly at anything for thirty minutes.

Acting First Sergeant Henry ordered the soldiers to fall in and fill their canteens with water. He led 156 armed soldiers toward Houston's jail on Capital and Bagby Streets by way of Brunner Avenue continuing

along San Felipe Street, past Montrose and stopped near Valentine Street in the San Felipe District. During their two-hour march on the city, the soldiers killed fifteen whites, including four policemen, and seriously wounded twelve others, one of whom, a policeman, subsequently died.

Four Colored soldiers were also killed. Two soldiers were shot by friendly fire in camp and on San Felipe Street. The soldiers' mistakenly killed Captain Joseph Mattes of the Illinois National Guard because they thought he was a police officer. Forty-two-year-old Sergeant Vida Henry was found lying on the grass along the Southern Pacific Railroad tracks by a squad of the Illinois National Guard ½ mile south of San Felipe Road and Southern Pacific Crossing on August 24, 1917. According to the ambulance driver, Lincoln Kennerly, the soldiers notified Coroner Sid Westheimer Company at 7:30am. Henry D. Goldberg, Sid Westheimer Undertaking embalmer, examined Sergeant Vida Henry's body. In Goldberg's sworn statement on August 24, 1917, Sergeant Henry's skull had been badly crushed with a blunt instrument and he had a five-inch-deep knife or bayonet wound ranging from his left clavicle to his heart.

The military indicted 118 enlisted men of 24th Infantry for their participation in the mutiny and riot. 110 soldiers were found guilty. Ninety-one soldiers were convicted by the courts and sentenced 2 years to life, four soldiers were killed during the riot as previously mentioned, seven acquitted, one withdrawn on account of insanity, and nineteen were hung.

However, the events and actions taken against Houston's Colored citizens after the incident are the most horrifying and terrifying racial and physical injustices enforced in the history of the city. After the incident, the city was placed under martial law which continued for a number days arming whites with weapons to protect their homes and disarming and unjustly arresting Colored citizens. To escape the brutality and harsh treatment by the city of Houston's police force and other whites, Colored citizens sold their homes and possessions at a loss and migrated north. According to one physician interviewed by Gruening, *having a home is all right, but not when you never know when you leave it in the morning if you will really be able to get back to it that night. 130 colored people left in one day. In June, one labor agent exported more than nine hundred Negroes to points along the Pennsylvania Railroad (pg 17, 1917).*

NAACP

The Houston Riot of 1917 was the catalyst for the establishment of the NAACP Houston Chapter. On August 23, 1917, Martha Gruening, NAACP Assistant Secretary traveled to Houston, Texas to investigate the Houston Riot of 1917 that involved 156 African American soldiers of the 3rd Battalion 24th Infantry station at Camp Logan. While investigating, she found the time ripe for organizing a NAACP Houston Chapter.

The primary cause of the Houston Riot was the habitual brutality of the white police officers of Houston in their treatment of Colored people (Martha Gruening, Houston An NAACP Investigation 1917).

Soon after Gruening's Houston visit, postal worker, M.B. Patten called a meeting of Houston's leading Colored professionals, clergymen, and businessmen. The application was filed by Clifton F. Richardson and thus the NAACP Houston Chapter was established May 31, 1918. Henry L. Mims was the first president of the Houston and Harris County NAACP and Richardson served as Secretary.

Colored Branch
1918-1935

711 Prairie Avenue
806 Clay Avenue
603 Prairie Avenue
417 West Dallas Avenue
1209 Bagby Street
1217 Bagby Street

In 1905, L.H. Spivey, T.M. Fairchild, E.O. Smith, and several Negro leaders meet with William A. Hunton the National Colored Secretary to discuss establishing a Houston YMCA for Negroes. These Houston leaders continued to meet on Sundays for many years; however, their initial quest to establish a Y failed until the National War Work Council established the Colored Soldiers and Sailors Branch of Houston Young Men's Christian Associations of the United States in 1918.

Lincoln Theatre
711 Prairie Avenue
Houston, Texas 77004

The Colored YMCA

The Colored YMCA of Houston opened in February 1918 under the National War Work Council, Young Men's Christian Associations of the United States. The Colored Soldiers and Sailors Branch of Houston Young Men's Christian Association (YMCA) was housed on the third floor of the Lincoln Theatre under the leadership of Professor Howard Payne Carter to provide fraternal and Christian fellowship for Houston's Colored soldiers and sailors returning from World War I. During the first year of service, the Y secured over 400 jobs, 740 bonuses of $60 each, 943 letters written for soldiers attempting to secure allotments overdue parents, raised $200 from Colored churches and business firms for expenses, organized one boys' club, furnished free pens, ink, and paper to all returning soldiers. In March 1919, a group of citizens both white and Colored concerned about the closing of many local agencies for military personnel met in the Colored Carnegie Library at 1112 Fredrick Street to establish a permeant organization, the Colored Branch of Houston Young Men's Christian Association with a $100 per month stipend from the Central Association under the leadership of General Secretary Page.

Professor Howard Payne Carter, Tennessee native, was the first Executive Secretary. The Board of

Directors and Officers were Reverend E.H. Holden, Chairman; C.F. Richardson, Vice Chairman; O.P. DeWalt, Treasurer; L.O. Lockett, Secretary; G.H. Webster, Chairman of the Finance Committee; J.R. Burdett, Dr. F.F. Stone, Reverend H.D. Greene, Frank L. Lane, Professor James D. Ryan, T.M. Fairchild, Reverend G.B. Young, Reverend C.K. Brown, Attorney S.H. Cavitt, J.H. Branch, Reverend J.H. Douglass, and J.W. Hubert.

The Y grew rapidly. By 1920, teachers were secured for the Y night school and arrangements were made with the Colored Library to have a circulating branch in the Y building. The Y offered many programs and services including free employment services, game rooms, reading rooms, men and boys membership bible clubs, HI-Y Clubs, football, tennis, basketball, volleyball, track, noon hour socials, banquets, debates, concerts, swimming, and noon day meetings at industrial plants. The Y eventually outgrew its space in the Lincoln Theatre building located at 711 Prairie Avenue and needed a larger facility.

1920 Rapid Growth

The Y's rapid growth and lack of space made it imperative for the organization to expand to a larger facility located at 806 Clay Avenue. Mr. DeFrantz, C.H. Tobias, William C. Craver, E.L. Gordon, Max Yergan, and J.B. Watson visited the Colored Y in April 1920 to survey the economic situation of Colored people and the state of race relations. The Y received a positive recommendation. As a result, Julius Rosenwald notified the Colored Branch of Houston YMCA office that he would give $25,000 on a $100,000 building.

In 1921, with the assistance of W.C. Paige, General Secretary of the Central Association and Dr. J.W. Slaughter of the Houston Foundation, the Colored YMCA received a substantial appropriation from the Community Chest Fund to helped ensure the success of the expansion. The Y's Membership Drive and Building Campaign to raise funds to secure a larger facility started on February 22, 1921 with a special event, YMCA Tag Day. The White YMCA pledged to match the $3,000 raised by the Colored YMCA with a $2,000 matching gift. Professor E.L. Gordon State Secretary of the Colored Men's Department attended the event. The Colored YMCA of Houston secured over $300,000 in funding for programming prior to the Membership Drive and Building Campaign KicKoff. $178,000 was allocated for veterans and $120,000 for war risk insurance.

Carter Resigns

Professor Howard Payne Carter resigned his position as Executive Secretary after serving three years in May 1921 due to the white board's hostile and prejudicial opposition to Editor C.F. Richardson serving on the Colored YMCA of Houston's Board of Management. Assistant Secretary Hubert Lott was appointed the Executive Secretary pro tem on probation and his first assignment was to collect the pledges from the big Membership Drive. Chairman Hardeway made it clear that the Colored Board of Management would not allow the Houston YMCA White Board of Directors to dictate to them who should be elected as officers of the Colored Y. As a result, the Colored YMCA Board of Management voted unanimously to end all relations with the white board because they refused to serve under the *big stick* policy of the White YMCA Board. The Colored Board of Management believed the white board's despotic and kaiseristic policy and attitude was unacceptable. The Colored Board of Management meet on Thursday, January 25, 1923 at Carnegie Library with the E.L. Gordon the Negro of the State YMCA work and W.C. Paige of the white Y to finalize the reorganization of the Colored Y. The following were present at the reorganization meeting L.V. Harrison, E.O. Woolfolk, S.W. Johnson, J.I. Donaldson, Reverend B. Belcher, L.H. Spivey, J.J. Hardeway, S.H. Cavitt, G.B.M. Turner, N.G. Henderson, R.G. Lockett, Herbert Lott, Dr F.F. Stone, L. Lacy, and R.M. Catching.

Many members doubled and tripled their contributions to ensure the Y's success to operate on an independent basis-manned, managed, operated, and financed exclusively by members of the Colored race. Former Executive Secretary H.P. Carter pledged to devote his spare moments gratuitously to the local Y's work.

Inter Church Boys' and Young Men's Council
On Sunday, October 24, 1923, the YMCA sponsored a mass father-son meeting at the Knights of Pythias Hall on Swartz Street in Fifth Ward. R.G. Lockett addressed ministers to make an appeal to the fathers to join the Y's Inter Church Boys' and Young Men's Council. The Steering committee members were R.M. Catchings, E.O. Smith, Reverend J.I. Donaldson, L.H. Spivey. The Baptist Ministers' Union-Reverend E.O. Woolfolk, President voted the union's support in their regular meeting on October 7, 1923. The Boys' Secretary was W.D. Blair. The YMCA facility was located at 806 Clay Avenue.

YMCA Expansion Program
In 1924, the Colored Branch of Houston YMCA moved to a larger facility in downtown Houston in a three-story brick leased building opposite the Model Laundry on Smith Street and 603 Prairie Avenue.

The organization's leadership signed a 5-year lease agreement. Local churches provided final assistance to help furnish the rooms. The cost to provide furnishings for the first, second, and three floors was $2,000. The following churches pledged $80 each: Bethel Baptist, Pastor J.R. Burdett; Antioch Baptist, Reverend E.L. Harrison; Saint John Baptist, Reverend H.R. Johnson; Mount Zion Baptist, Reverend T.D. Hawkins; and Mount Vernon CME, Reverend G.E.D. Belcher. According to President J.J. Hardeway of the board, the $80 was sufficient enough to cover the costs of the smaller bedrooms. All donors who contributed $10 or more names were published to acknowledge their gift and to say thank you for supporting the Y's mission to improve the religious, social, moral, physical, and intellectual condition of young men and boys.

The Board of Directors J.J. Hardeway, President; Reverend J.I. Donaldson, Vice President; Robert Merritt Catchings, Recording Secretary; E.O. Smith, Treasurer; Dr. F.F. Stone, Reverend J.R. Burdett, L.H. Spivey, Reverend P.H. Watkins, Anderson Lacy, G.H. Webster, R.H. Lockett, J.P. Jones, and R.T. Andrews hired YMCA Springfield College Graduate, Felix C. Thurmond, as the Executive Secretary.

The Y moved to 417 West Dallas Avenue after the expiration of the 5-year lease.

Colored YMCA Camp for Boys

Gilbert T. Stocks took the helm as the Executive Secretary in 1926. Under Stocks leadership, the Y started the Colored YMCA Camp for Boys in 1927. On July 28, 1928, E.O. Smith conducted the Y's second year two-week camp for 25 boys. Each member of the board was required to volunteer for one day to help carryout programming and be present onsite in case of emergencies. Before entering camp, the boys were required to have a physical and dental exam. The camp's curriculum focus was on religion, education, and camp life.

The Hunton Young Men's Club of the YMCA

The Hunton Young Men's Club of the YMCA was organized on December 4, 1928. The club officers were President A.J. Turner, Secretary J.C. Collins, Treasurer S.H. McClain, Chaplain S.H. McClain, and Sergeant of Arms A.J. Henderson. In 1930, Haran J. Battle was hired to assist the executive secretary. The YMCA building was located at 417 West Dallas Avenue from 1928-30. The Colored Y offered the following activities including a Club for Caddies at River Oaks, hikes, games, playground activities at Bethlehem Settlement House, three senior high school Hi Y

TIMELINE 1928

January 16, 1928
Board members- H.P. Carter Chairman, J.F. Gomez, R.G. Lockett, Homer E. McCoy, and G.T. Stocks appointed to give special attention to Hi Y work in three high schools

December 11, 1928
Y Membership and Financial Drive

January 8, 1929
Hunton Young Men's Club of the YMCA meeting

February 2, 1929
Y Basketball Game at Emancipation Park Prairie View Panthers versus Y Crescents (The Y won 22-17)
Outstanding Players: Y Dezon, Holland, Codwell, and Sholders
PV Bates, Adams, and Anderson

August 14-23, 1929
Third Annual Colored YMCA Camp for Boys

January 10, 1930
Y Tigers defeated Prairie View Panthers 21-17 in basketball
Outstanding Players: Y Dezon, Holland, and Bradley; PV Howard, Collins, and Waller

February 14, 1930
Y Observe Negro History Week at the Y building at 417 West Dallas Avenue

March 24, 1930
Y Membership Drive

April 5, 1930
Three Y Hi clubs and two church delegations attended the State Older Boys' Conference in Marshall, Texas

April 13, 1930
Youth and Life Forum for Hi Y boys 417 West Dallas Avenue
Roy Hopkins from Wheatley High School pianist

Clubs, World War Service Bureau serving over 1,400 War Veterans since January 1, 1930, free employment bureau for men and boys, seasonal athletic sports, weekly meetings at industrial plants, men's dormitory, providing ushers for public meetings, supervision of the Negro Knot Holo Gang, and summer camp. The Y was also responsible for maintaining community organizations for young men, and other community activities. James D. Ryan, J.T. Donaldson, J.W. Herbert, F.F. Stone, and P.C. Colvin were elected to the Board of Directors on April 22, 1930.

The Colored YMCA Joins the Houston YMCA

From 1918-1920, the Colored Branch YMCA of Houston was part of the Houston YMCA; however, 1921-1931 it was an independent organization. On November 7, 1930, Dr. C.H. Tobias, Senior Secretary, National Council of the Colored Men's Department YMCA of North America visited the Colored Y to confer with key men about the Houston situation urging the leadership and community to join the movement to polarize the work of the local body. Stressing Houston's need for the services of a virile YMCA.

In February 1931, F.C. Fields General Secretary of the Central Association encouraged the Colored Branch of Houston YMCA to resume its relationship with the general Houston association and join the National Council YMCA and the Houston YMCA to give the Colored Branch an opportunity for access to resources to provide better quality and equal services to meet the needs of Houston's large and growing Negro population.

The Colored YMCA joined with the Houston YMCA in 1931 under the leadership of Tolmer F. Frazier and Board Chairman Dr. French F. Stone. As a result, the Colored Branch of Houston YMCA's Board of Directors once again became a Committee of Management.

New Y Head

In August 1931, William Curtis Craver became the Executive Secretary charged with implementing the changes in structure and operations of the developing YMCA. Craver was recruited by General Secretary of the Houston Association F.C. Fields and a small lay committee from the Colored YMCA to come and expand the Y's work in Houston. Before Craver arrived, the Colored YMCA was supervised by the executive secretary and a lay committee of 11 members. The branch also had one female secretary. There were only 100 members, one boy's club, and very few other programs. The Y was operating in a small three room rented quarters on Prairie and Smith. The depression had eroded the Colored Y's funding drastically resulting in services being cut.

TIMELINE 1931

April 22, 1930
James D. Ryan, J.T. Donaldson, J.W. Herbert, F.F. Stone, and P.C. Colvin elected to the board

August 30, 1930
4th Annual Summer Boys' Camp at Spring Creek

Haran J. Battle Camp Director

November 7, 1930
Dr. C.H. Tobias, Senior Secretary, National Council urges the Colored Y leadership to join the movement to polarize the work of the local body

February 28, 1931
F.C. Fields General Secretary encourages the Colored Branch to resume its relationship with the general Houston Association

September 1931
Camp at Spring Creek

William Curtis Craver
YMCA Executive Secretary

Colored Branch 1936-941

1217 Bagby Street

1932-1941

During his 18-year tenure, William Curtis Craver lead the Colored YMCA with great success through the Great Depression and World War II. The Great Depression of 1929-39 was the most extensive and lasting economic decline in the history of the Western industrialized world. The United States Stock Market crashed October 29, 1929, which sent Wall Street into a panic and wiped out millions of investors. The Great Depression had a devastating impact on the Colored YMCA; however, within one-year Craver was able to turn the organization in a thriving and successful Y. Craver established a lay committee of 150 volunteer lay committeemen supervising 15 divisions of work representing every section of Houston and every section of society.

The 15 divisions included the following: work for boys, service for industrial workers, a more widespread religious work, enlarged education and publicity, physical division, a program for foreign work, financial section, and interracial work for the city and state, a more comprehensive and united effort among the churches, a social and headquarters committee, a committee on leadership personnel and permanent membership organization. He also set up Junior College student associations aimed at developing the students' all-around leadership skills.

The Committee of Management under the leadership of Dr. F.F. Stone elected the following 1931 committee members to head up the initial 12 divisions:

Religious Work	Reverend J.I. Donaldson
Interracial	Professor J.D. Ryan
Educational	Dr. W.J. Howard and Professor R.M. Catchings
Physical	Professor J.E. Codwell
Interchurch	Professor E.O. Smith
Boys Work	Professor R.G. Lockett
Industrial	Miles W. Jordan and P.C. Colvin
Membership	H.P. Carter and G.H. Webster
Social and House	H.E. McCoy
Finance	O.J. Polk associated with E.O. Smith and J.W. Hubert

The General Director of Membership Howard Payne Carter along with five major directors that presided over the workers in the Wards.

The Ward Directors

Third Ward	Dr. I.K. Darby
Fifth Ward	C.C. Penn
Second Ward	Ray Williams
Fourth Ward	Walter Hurd
First and Sixth Ward	Dr. R.H.

Each director had a number of captain directors who lead various groups of his Ward.

YMCA Inclusive Membership Drive Campaign
Set for Life
April 24-May 3, 1932

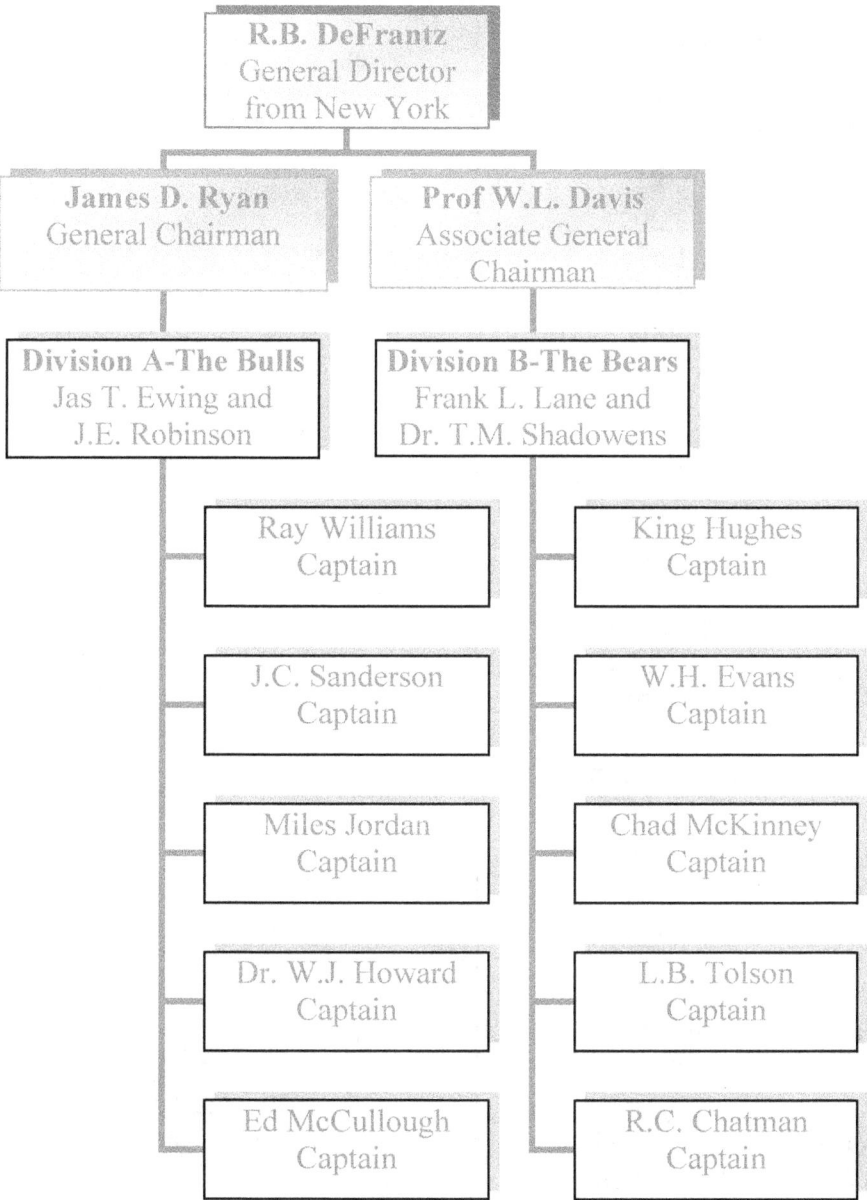

There are five workers assigned to each captain. The Church Co-Operation Chairman Reverend W.M. Sykes and a lay representative were assigned to visit each church to appeal to each minister of the city to touch upon the needs of the youth. The 1932 *Set for Life* Membership Campaign was the first inclusive membership campaign that the Colored Branch participated in with the Houston Association.

TIMELINE 1932

November 8-10, 1931
Membership Drive to increase membership and extend programs to all parts of the city

January 6, 1932
Julius Rosenwald died suddenly

The YMCA Association flag to be flown at half-mast for 30 days out of respect for Julius Rosenwald who gave over $600,000 to encourage Y work amongst the Negro people of the United States.

April 24-May 3, 1932
YMCA First Inclusive Membership Drive Campaign *Set for Life*

July 23, 1932
80 boys attend summer camp in Spring, Texas

October 1, 1932
Founders Day Celebration
Observation of Sir Williams Anniversary opens the Houston Negro YMCA Fall Membership Campaign *On to School Movement*

Dr. W.M. Drake General Director assisted by Ed McCullough
H.P. Carter Membership Director of the Drive

The Founder's Day Committee
W.J. Howard, Chairman
Jesse C. McDade and Dr. R.H. Ward

October 4, 1932
Schools for commercial law, shorthand, typewriting opens

October 11, 1932
Founders Day Celebration

June 24, 1933
Y Camp Spring Creek, Texas
Vacation Clubs 18 elementary schools
Y Club Hikes at Green's Bayou

Under Craver's leadership, the Colored YMCA grew rapidly ranking Houston Colored YMCA first for quality and volume of programs and services to men and boys in the state of Texas in the 1932 YMCA Yearbook.

The following list below are highlights from Craver's first year of service as Executive Secretary:

1932 Division Highlight Accomplishments

New Members	825
Students Stimulated in Missionary Thinking	3,209
Boys trained in camp, weekend hikes, and clubs	1,525
Father and Son Observance Week	3,165
Personal problems, employment, and relief	400
State Conference	75
Inspirational and Religious Programs	5,565
Industrial Centers	1,357
Athletic Programs	2,892

On September 24, 1932, the Y launched the Camp Saving Club. The club was designed to help boys save $.10 per week for fifty weeks to ensure they had a six-dollar scholarship in camp for 1933. The *On to School Movement* was promoted by the YMCA and Chamber of Commerce in order to teach boys how to thrift.

On October 4, 1932, The Colored YMCA opened schools in commercial law, shorthand, and typing under the leadership of the Committee of Education for men and women who wished to benefit from the opportunity. Classes were held nightly at 1209 Bagby Street at the Colored YMCA headquarters.

By 1933, the white collar group was no longer the backbone of the organization. The YMCA Growth and Trends of the movement had changed.

The Father & Son Observance Week was organized in 1933 with over 509 fathers and sons. At the end of the weeklong event, a Father and Son Banquet was held for 200 fathers and sons at Jack Yates High School.

TIMELINE 1933

July 8, 1933
100 boys attend summer camp in Spring, Texas

August 12, 1933
National Laymen's Conference of the YMCA's Program in the Light of Present Trends

October 5, 1933
Set Up Conference
Special talks to discuss the problems facing the YMCA. General Secretary Fields and Norman Macleod City Wide Boys Secretary will present the message. to Colored prominent leaders both in the YMCA and community, ministers, Colored YMCA leadership including the 14 division Chairmen and subcommittees

October 7, 1933
Founders Day Program to honor the memory of the founder of the YMCA Sir George Williams 112th Anniversary of his birth.

October 11-November 11, 1933
Special Membership Renewal Program

October 21, 1933
National Secretary F.T. Wilson, national student secretary of the Y visits several high schools to speak to students and answer their questions about world peace and interracial goodwill

December 4, 1933
Citywide Religious Institute and Training Conference of Church Workers

November 4, 1933
3 day Hi Y Conference *Making Leaders for Today and Tomorrow*

November 25, 1933
400 attend the YMCA's Men and Mission Sunday at Wesley Chapel

Hi Y Conference at Prairie View University

1934 Division Highlight Accomplishments

711 meetings in all divisions touching	27,622
110 religious gatherings	3,284
90 athletic events	2,382
45 meetings of an educational nature	1,888
412 boys' meetings	17,762
Religious conference in Dallas	78

1935 Division Highlight Accomplishments

Summer camp	150
Fathers & Sons Observation Week	700
Boys Religious Training Conferences	300
Employment and Relief	406
Delinquent boys helped	71
Supervised 21 Y Clubs	880
Free movies and entertainment for	367
Religious meeting at 28 stations	3,020
Physical department	131
Athletic Programs	3,000
Volunteers 15 divisions-57 major projects	144

TIMELINE 1934

March 6-9, 1934
2nd Annual Father & Son Observance Week

John Rice visits Houston to present President Roosevelt's Social Security Program and feature of the Employment Insurance measure being debated to Congress and the nation

March 9, 1934
Father & Son Banquet at Wheatley High School

April 7, 1934
100 attend Y Annual Dinner at the Odd Fellows Temple

May 19, 1934
YMCA Membership Campaign to recruit 500 new members

July 3-August 3, 1934
Summer Camp of Promise

July 1, 1934
3rd Annual Educational and Inspirational Camp

50 boys leave for camp

September 22, 1934
Y Officers Election
F.F. Stone, Chairman
Frank L. Lane, Vice Chairman
R.M. Catchings, Recording Secretary
J.C. Sanings

November 10, 1934
Y Financial Membership Drive

December 8, 1934
Y conducts drive to support missionaries

February 23, 1935
J.C. Rice speaks at program

April 26, 1935
Y Sons and Dads Banquet

The Houston Negro Chamber of Commerce

The Houston Negro Chamber of Commerce is the second oldest Black Chamber of Commerce in the country. The Chamber was organized in September 1935 by several prominent community leaders, Joseph E. Robinson, A. White, C.A. Shaw, Dr. F.F. Stone, R.O'Hara Lanier, C. Crouch, C.F. Richardson, C.W. Rice, L.H. Spivey, Sr., M. Thomas, H.P. Carter, F.L. Lane, Dr. W.M. Drake, M.W. Jordan, G.A. Crawford, G.O. Burgess, Dr. C.W. Pemberton, R.R. Grovey, and J. E. Henry, to promote the civic, economic, industrial, agricultural, and social welfare of Houston Negro citizens; encourage a larger patronage of Negro enterprises and practical education in the trades and arts to stimulate better business; and develop a more amicable relationship between racial groups.

The first president was J.E. Robinson, Sr.

TIMELINE 1935

May 4, 1935
Spring Campaign to recruit 500 new members

May 25, 1935
Spring Membership Campaign over the top 521 new members

July 2, 1935-August 10, 1935
Y Summer Camp

F.F. Stone retires as YMCA Chairman after serving in a leadership capacity of the Colored YMCA for 17 years. He was the Chairman for 9 years. Frank L. Lane, Vice Chairman appointed Chairman.

October 5, 1935
Y holds Set Up Conference

October 12, 1935
Friends of the Y honor F.F. Stone at William C. Craver's home

November 2, 1935
5th Annual Membership Renewal Program

November 18, 1935
Marion McMillan attends Racial Cooperation Banquet for all College YMCA and YWCA in downtown Houston

November 23, 1935
Y raises $100 for African Work

LET'S THINK MORE BOYS

Thinking is important business of the world, and a determining factor in the affairs of men

FOURTEENTH ANNUAL SESSION OF
The State Older Boys' Conference
DALLAS, TEXAS
Moorland Branch Y. M. C. A.
MARCH 29, 30, 31, 1935

Conference Theme--Working with God in Building a New World

Dr. M. W. Dogan
President Wiley College, Marshall, Texas; Chairman State Committee Colored Work Department

S. H. Fowler, Sr.
Ex. Secy. Colored Branch Y. M. C. A., Fort Worth, Texas; Director of Conference

R. W. Bullock
National Council, N. Y. Co-operating Executive

W. C. Craver
Ex. Secy. Colored Branch, Houston, Texas--Director Discussion Group Leaders

May your thinking and acting be in line with the supreme will and chief desire of the Universal Mind

Dr. J. W. Anderson, M. D.,
Dallas, Texas
Chairman Endowment Dept.

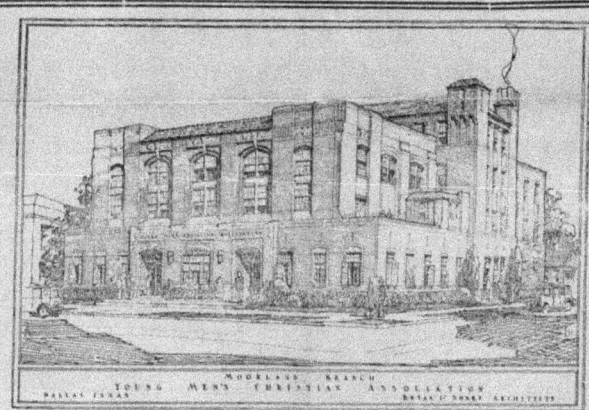
Moorland Branch Young Men's Christian Association, Dallas, Texas
The Finest Building in the Southwest, where some of the finest finished products for Service are produced.

J. H. Henry
Dallas, Texas
State Secretary, Texas Young Men's Christian Association

Thinking regulates conduct and action, introduces the distinction between right and wrong and works for human benefit and enlightment

Thinking Boys – Ambitious Boys – Aspiring Boys – Boys who are helping to build a New World

REGISTRATION
Delegates include Boys of Schools and Colleges, Hi-Y Clubs, Fraternal Organizations, Employed Boys' Clubs, and Young Peoples' Societies, Adult Workers with Boys, School and Sunday School Officials, Club Leaders, Committeemen and Directors—All invited to register and participate (write for enrollment cards) Enrollment Fee $1.00. Room and Board $1.50 for the 3 days.

Entertainment and Other Interesting Features
Free Banquet, Varied Recreational Activities and Educational Tour. As usual quartets from many cities will furnish music at times to the delight of all. Delegates from different cities shall compete in competitive games and recreational activities.

Auspices of Executive Committee. Texas Young Men's Christian Association, 303 Y. M. C. A. Building, Dallas, Texas: J. H. Henry, State Secretary; G. C. Good, Boys' Work Secretary; M. W. Dogan, Marshall, Chairman Executive Committee, Colored Department; S. H. Fowler, Sr., 603 Jones Street, Fort Worth, Director of Conference.

NATHANIEL HARDEN, Dallas, President   GEORGE DURHAM, Fort Worth, Sec'y.

Record Year 1935

In 1935, the Colored YMCA closed with a record year since its establishment in 1918.

1935 Division Highlight Accomplishments
Athletic Events 47 touching men and boys	3,047
Father and Son Observance Week	7,052
Father and Son Banquet	553
Rosenwald Sunday under joint program with the YWCA touching men and women	760
Membership 700 percent increase in 4 years	850
Summer Boys Camp Spring Creek	130
Camp Boys Saving Club boys sent themselves to camp	40
21 Y Clubs embracing a membership of college, high school, and elementary school boys	1,100
State Older Boys Conference in Dallas	78
3 Day Training Conference to train boys to lead their club	3
Conference enrollment	185

The Week of Prayer in cooperation with the World Committee of the YMCA conducted prayer and discussions at 43 centers led by 45 volunteers totaling 98 sessions bringing over 500 men together at East Trinity Church. Thirty-seven churches of Protestant and Catholic Faiths made up the meetings.

The Y Clubs raised $100 for the support of Max Yergen, Y Secretary in South Africa. The Negro History Committee, Youth Movements, and Community Chest all were very important components of the Colored YMCA. Programming also included Relief, Employment Work through schools and movies, socials, award nights, cooperation with the local Negro Health Committee and the YWCA.

Father and Son Banquet

Industrial Division Committee Meeting

1936 Colored YMCA Elected Officers
F.L. Lane, Branch Chairman
Jesse C. McDade, Vice Chairman
J.S. Sanderson, Recording Secretary
R.A. Williams, Assistant Recording Secretary

14 Departments of Work Appointed

Branch membership	Jesse C. McDade and Solon Brandon
Religious	Reverend J.S. Scott
Education	J.E. Armstead
Industrial	M.W. Jordan and R.H. Guess
Physical	H.P. Carter
New building and agencies	W.E. Miller
Finance	James T. Ewing
Interracial	James D. Ryan
Camps	Dr. F.F. Stone
Socials and housing	R.A. Williams
Foreign Y Work	E.O. Smith
Young men's programs	Chas A. Shaw
Employment and Relief	T.M. Fairchild
Boys Work	J.C. Sanderson

Program Honoring Abraham Lincoln

On February 12, 1936, Fritz Cansler, former Secretary of the Denver YMCA and Secretary of the Dallas YMCA, spoke at the Colored YMCA's program honoring Abraham Lincoln at the Odd Fellows Temple. Cansler, well known for his YMCA work in education, was introduced by William C. Craver. Cansler stayed at Mr. and Mrs. H.P. Carter's home during his stay. Other program speakers were Chas A. Shaw, Secretary of the Houston Negro Chamber of Commerce, W.L. Davis, Principal Harper Junior High School, Frank L. Lane, President Houston Postal Alliance, C.W. Rice, Negro Labor News, and Albert White representing Negro youth.

1936 Division Highlight Accomplishments

Membership	1,000
Seven High School Hi Y Clubs	430
Twelve Elementary School Gra Y Clubs	720
Summer Camp at Spring, Texas	150
Religious meetings at 28 locations	1,500
Father and Son Observance Week	3,500
Father and Son 5th Annual Banquet	600
Physical Department	110
Camp Boys Saving Club boys sent themselves to camp	40
Training and Religious Conferences	200
International Alliance Men and Religion Sunday	600
Educational Division	1,000

The Y Clubs raised $100 for Association Africa Work

Hall of Fame

In April 1936, the Houston YMCA established the Hall of Fame to recognize men that excel in services to the branch in the Membership Department. A large photo of the men selected for the Hall of Fall was displayed at the Y association office in the trophy room. The Colored Y Membership Department voted to place the following men in the Hall of Fame for the successful leadership of previous campaigns James Delbridge Ryan, Dr William Marcellus Drake, Frank L. Lane, Rollin Lee Isaacs, James Charles Sanderson and for unusual service in selling memberships during the past year Solon Brandon, James Calhoun, and Dr. F.F. Stone were selected.

TIMELINE 1936

February 22, 1936
State Committee of the YMCA meets at local branch and William Craver elected as Director of the 1937 Older Boys Conference

February 22, 1936
Y Tigers win and lose in Houston double header

March 13, 1936
700 attend 4th Annual Father and Son Banquet held at the Pilgrim Temple

Wheatley High Cages defeat YMCA Quintet

March 27-29, 1936
Older Boys Conference in Galveston Directors for the State Older Boys give program dean R.O. Lanier to deliver the address

April 24, 1936
2nd Annual Dinner at the Pilgrim Temple and Fritz Cansler Executive of the Moorland Branch YMCA of Dallas chief speaker

July 14, 1936
Twenty Informer Newsboys attend YMCA Camp in Spring, Texas

August 8, 1936
Y Summer Camp a great success 135 campers, 200 visitors during the 23-day session

September 19, 1936
YMCA Officers for new year elected

November 1, 1936
Houston Y Forum third meeting and forum sponsored jointly by the YMCA and YWCA *The Moral Aspect of Marriage*

Hall of Fame

The Board of Management and Membership Department Committee voted in April 17, 1937 to place all successful General Chairmen of Annual Membership Campaigns in the YMCA Hall of Fame niche at the Association Headquarters

James Delbridge Ryan
1932 General Chairman

Dr. William Marcellus Drake
1932 Fall General Chairman

Frank L. Lane
1933 General Chairman

Rollin Lee Isaacs
1935 General Chairman

James Charles Sanderson
1935 General Chairman

W. Leonard Davis
1936 General Chairman

TIMELINE 1937

December 4-6, 1936
Y Institute held at PV *Making Leaders Tomorrow* slogan for 100 delegates *Forward with Negro Youth*

The Institute was designed to give special training for the groups assembled to kindle a new spirit and enthusiasm for YMCA Work amongst Negroes

January 30, 1937
Sixth Annual Negro State Older Boys Conference *In Spite of Handicaps* held in Austin, Texas

January 31, 1937
Y Joint Forum on the Social Security Act January 31, 1937 held in the social hall of the YWCA first lecture given by Chas A. Shaw

February 1, 1937
Boxing and wrestling classes open

February 6, 1937
Basketball program set up with two teams

March 5, 1937
5th Annual Father and Son Banquet held in Pilgrim Building auditorium over 500 fathers and sons attended

April 2-4, 1937
Sixth Annual Negro State Older Boys Conference *In Spite of Handicaps* held in Austin, Texas

March 6, 1937
Tillotson defeats Houston YMCA Raiders 39 to 20

April 16, 1937
Annual Dinner in the Pilgrim Temple address delivered by Edward L. Snyder, Representative of The Universal Life Insurance Company and Ray Williams Event Chairman

1937 Unusual Service in Selling Memberships
Solon Brandon

Dr. French F. Stone   James M. Calhoun

Set Up Conference

The Colored YMCA *Set Up Conference* was held in the branch's auditorium for the 15 department 150 working committee members who served on various committees on September 26, 1936. Conference speakers were President W.R. Banks, Professor Lee C. Phillips, Prairie View College, Grover C. Good, State Y Secretary, Dallas, General Secretary F.C. Fields, and Jack Roe leader of Young Men's Work of Texas.

Membership Campaign Division Committee Meeting

Membership Campaign

The Colored YMCA's Sixth Annual Inclusive YMCA Membership Campaign was led by Dean R.O. Lanier and L.H. Spivey.

Division Managers
The Bears E.L. Synder and Archie Wells
Captains Bears Alphonse Mills, F.F. Stone, N. Dudley A.W. Tinner, E.F. Jones, W.M. Sweeny, and Leonard Thomas

The Bulls J.E. Gooden and L.J. Mann
Captains Bulls J.M. Calhoun, M. Batteau, W. Green, M. Robinson, S.L. Payne, J.M. Busby, and Gus Harris

Little Bulls and Little Bears of Harrisburg lead by Reverend J.R. Robinson

Boys R.L. Isaacs and W.L. Davis

Industrial R.H. Guess, J.A. Scott, M.W. Jordan, and J.C. Sanderson

TIMELINE 1937

May 7, 1937
Victory Dinner

May 15, 1937
Membership Drive Excels 680 members enrolled cash $1,300

The Bulls won the Silver and Gold Crowns in the number of memberships and money reported

Elementary Loving Cup won by the Gra Y of the Douglass School

June 26, 1937
Annual YMCA Summer Camp opens on July 2, 1937 over 400 boys applied to attend the 10-day camp

July 14, 1937
Y Camp second session directed by former camp boy and Meharry Medical College medical student, Sidney Smith assisted by Vernon Punch Wheatley High School graduate, Joseph Harris student at Prairie View, Carl Mack graduate of Houston College, John L Blount, Jr. student at Wiley College, Ceil Jordan Prairie View, and Robert Haynes Jack Yates High School.

October 27-29, 1937
Y Training Conference *Getting Set for life's Race* at Wheatley High School

21 Y Clubs attending J.C. Sanderson Chairman of Boys Work Department

October 30, 1937
Camp 150
Fathers and Son 3,052
28 religious meetings touching 1,000 young men and boys
Furnished employment for 50 men
Training camp 200
Athletics 1,000
20 Y Clubs bi weekly meetings 1,400

Langston Elementary Football Team with Principal George R. Munline on right and Y member on the left

H.M. Washington presents trophy to sponsor, David Bradford's Phillis Wheatley Hi Y Club

M.W. McDonald Physical Education Committee Chairman presents trophies to youth members

TIMELINE 1937

November 1-16, 1937
Seventh Annual Membership *Round Up* from Spring Campaign Effort Launched by the Colored Branch YMCA

November 6, 1937
Division leaders selected for Community Chest Drive

Rosenwald Fund spends $619,763 on rural schools

November 20, 1937
YMCA and YWCA sponsor a Vesper at the YWCA located at 506 Louisiana during the Observance of World Fellowship and Week of Prayer

December 10-12, 1937
The Second Annual YMCA Institute for the State of Texas held at Prairie View College

December 1, 1937
YMCA Gra Y and Hi Y raise $100 for support of the YMCA Work in South Africa

December 18, 1937
Spring Campaign Effort
Blues won from the standpoint of members and attendance

The Reds close in cash
Captain J.A. Scott won the silver cup
Captain Carl Mack close second

What has the Y done?

In 1937, the YMCA's membership department enrolled 2,163 boys and men. The organization's 14 departments of work service lead by 175 committeemen held 107 committee meetings, 549 committee meetings and various events staged by several departments involving total attendance of 38,870 persons-7,319 men, 22,781 boys, and 5,708 women.

The Gra Y Clubs held 251 meetings with attendance of 9,341 boys and approximately, 200 boys attended summer camp. Throughout the year the YWCA and YMCA cosponsored 20 forums. There were 88 religious meetings conducted with attendance of 4,337. The Father and Son Banquet and Week served 4,032.

Two Wheatley High School students, Club President John Richard Crear and Milton Williams, and Allen Ford, Jr., from Jack Yates High School were delegates at the Y Conference held in Marshall, Texas.

Rosenwald Exercise

Endowment Secretary of the Grand United Order of Odd Fellows J.W. Rice and Merrill E. Brown, Houston businessman and former secretary of the YMCA of the State of Florida were selected as the principal speakers of the 6th Annual Rosenwald Memorial held at Odd Fellows Temple on Sunday, February 6, 1938.

L.K. Shivery

The Colored YMCA added a new staff member, L.K. Shivery, to conduct boys work within the community. Shivery graduated from Morehouse College in Atlanta, Georgia. After graduation, he worked with boys in New York and Atlanta under the direction of the Urban League and Boy Scouts of America. Shivery's major responsibilities with these organizations were to guide communities at work, counsel individuals, promote club programs, camp and swim programming, coach amateur theatricals, and supervise various athletic groups. Hiring Shivery to conduct boys' work was the fulfillment of the Colored Branch's promise by board of management to add an additional staff.

Within a short time, Shivery established five new community center programs in Harrisburg, Houston, Highland Heights, Third Ward, and Fifth Ward. The new community center programs were designed to emphasize community work by

TIMELINE 1938

January 22, 1938
Yates' Basketeers Trounce Y Red Raiders, 35 to 14

YMCA Enrolls 2,163 Members in 1937

January 29, 1938
27,600 Votes For J.H. Jemison

Select Speakers for the Rosenwald Exercise

Boys' Work Secretary Added To YMCA Staff

February 5, 1938
Jemison Keeps In Front of Sweeney by 36,200 Votes

Dr. B.J. Covington Leaves Antioch and Joins Saint John

Rosenwald Program Scheduled Sunday

February 12, 1938
Informer Newsboys Hold Enthusiastic Meeting At the YMCA

February 19, 1938
YMCA To Pay Tribute To Dr. F.F. Stone

Dr. Drake Expected to Reach Goal of $1,000 in Two Weeks

Harrisburg Forms Y Committee

Indoor Games A New Feature of the Y

March 9, 1938
Booker T. Washington's Granddaughter Awarded A Scholarship

YMCA and YWCA Sponsor A Series of Social Lecture Groups

establishing play centers and organizing boys and young men into groups for the purpose of helping them to develop physically, mentally, and spiritually. The new Y Centers at Highland Heights School, Atherton School, Mt. Sinai Church, Houston Heights, Harrisburg School, and New Douglass School grounds, 3rd Ward were also used to enroll boys for camp, athletics, and other programming during the months of July, August, and September.

Dr. French Franklin Stone

On Sunday March 6, 1938, hundreds of community members from all walks of life gathered in the Odd Fellows Temple to pay homage and memorialize Dr. F.F. Stone through a special program on the first anniversary of his death. Dr. French Franklin Stone, Houston Doctor and former Chairman of the Negro Branch of the YMCA for many years laid the foundation of the Young Men's Christian Association among Negroes of Houston. All speakers told the same story as how Dr. Stone won men to the Y Program by his persistent efforts in never giving up and the high ground he took as a basis for interracial goodwill. Among those that took part in the memorialization were Professor W.L. Davis, Dr. O.L. Lattimore, J.W. Rice, Dr. H.E. Lee, Reverend S.A. Pleasants, Reverend J.S. Scott, and Gavin Ulmer, President of the YMCA. The audience sang two hymns with deep feeling, *Abide With Me* and *When Peace Like a River*. The Harmony Glee Club under the direction of Dr. P.D. Foster rendered several appropriate selections. J.W. Jones directed the congregational singing. The program was drawn up by Professors J.D. Ryan and E.O. Smith, and T.M. Fairchild. Frank L. Lane Chairman of the Colored Branch, presided.

Mae Turner, Joe Louis, and Clarence Muse

TIMELINE 1938

March 12, 1938
Citizens pay Tribute To Late Dr. F.F. Stone

March 16, 1938
James Wheldon Johnson to Dedicate Prairie Views Gym

Dedication of Prairie View Gym Draws Large Crowd

Says the Negro Came To America As Indentured Servants

March 19, 1938
The Y Opens Two Centers Emphasizes Community Activities

YMCA To Hold Dinner

YMCA To Sponsor Softball League

March 26, 1938
Trojans Win Y Tourney

Delinquent Work Among Girls and Boys

March 30, 1938
Mae Turner, Joe Louis, and Clarence Muse who have important roles in the spirit of youth a feature film of swing, song, and sock opening at the Lincoln Theatre Saturday night.

Attend Y Conference

April 2, 1938
Hi Y Club to Hold Open Forum

April 6, 1938
Jemison and Everett Head Y Campaign

April 9, 1938
YMCA Membership Campaign Will Be Launched April 25

April 16, 1938
Joint Y Program Is Held At Houston College

Announce YMCA Division Leaders

Houston College

The YMCA and YWCA groups of Houston College for Negroes presented a joint program at the regular chapel exercises on Wednesday April 12 in the Jack Yates High School auditorium.

Membership Campaign

The 4th Annual YMCA Dinner for Membership was held on Friday, April 15, 1938 in the YMCA assembly room under the leadership of Ray A. Williams, Chairman of Social Affairs. Freeman Everett and J.H. Jemison were named as leaders, General Directors, of the YMCA Seventh Annual Membership Campaign. They officially launched the 1938 Campaign on Tuesday, April 26 with a budget increase recommendation from Executive Secretary William C. Craver to serve 200 additional underprivileged boys by giving each boy a YMCA membership for the year at a rate of $1. *It will secure our leadership for the future as no other investment.*

Reverend L.H. Simpson Pastor of the Pleasant Hill Church was selected as Division Leader for the Bears and Reverend J.L. Robinson Pastor of the Asbury Church, Harrisburg for the Bulls. O.K. Manning (Bulls) and J.G. Pearsall (Bears) were assigned as their assistants.

Bears Division Leader, Reverend L.H. Simpson
- J.G. Pearsall, Assistant
- Captains Theo Thompson, Thomas Parr, A.W. Jackson, J.W. Peavy, and L.J. Mann.

Bulls Division Leader, Reverend J.L. Robinson
- O.K. Manning, Assistant
- Bulls Captains William Robinson, R.A. Williams, E.L. Snyder, C. Guidry, and G.T. McIntyre.

- Prospects: Associates William Sweeney
- Sustaining Memberships: Dr. P.W. Beal and Dr. Fred Parrot with the assistance of the Committee of the Drive.
- Club Solicitation: J.E. Armstead and William Ponder
  - Goal approach 65 clubs, socities, and other organizatons.
- School Section: Dean R.O. Lanier and L.H. Spivey
  - Captains R.L. Isaacs, J.C. Sanderson, J.E. Gooden, P.H. Holden, W.L.D. Johnson, W.J. Smith, A.E. Norton, Jr., Wendell Terrell, B.S. McMillan, and others

TIMELINE 1938

April 16, 1938
Attend Inauguration program of J.H. Jemison Bronze Mayor of Houston Monday Night April 18th Odd Fellows Temple Louisiana at Prairie

April 23, 1938
YMCA Launches Spring Drive

Leaders Named In Campaign 38,870 contacts made by the Y during the year.

May 7, 1938
YMCA Softball League Is Organized

May 28, 1938
Negro Appreciation Night Buffalo Stadium May 18, 1938 Under Auspices of Negro Chamber of Commerce

YMCA Drive Extended One Week

Y Campaign Goes Over In Great Drive

YMCA Softball League Schedule

District Meeting to Convene at Church of God

2nd and 3rd Ward Teams Play Friday

June 4, 1938
Bilbo Still Trying to have Negroes Shipped to Africa

June 11, 1938
White Vocational College Adopts Tuskegee Program

The first preliminary rally for enrolling boys for summer camp period July 1-11 will be held at the Y on June 10, 1938 at 8pm.

Third Ward Civic Club Holds Meeting at the Y

Summer Y Camps will open on July 1, 1938 with 60 boys attending session 1.

- Committee of Publicity: C.F. Richardson, Sr., Carter Wesley, and C.W. Rice
- Industrial Division Managers: M.W. Jordan and J.M. Mayo
    - Captains S.P. Smead, J.A. Scott, and Archie Wells and three others.
- The Longshoreman's Group under the direction of Freeman Everett and A.R. Spiller, and local directors at Ship Channel.

The Spring Membership Campaign was the most influential drive for members ever staged in Houston. On the closing night May 18, the goal of 50 members had been oversubscribed to the tune of 953 with $1,500 in cash and pledges by sustaining members of $200 making the total $1,600. The Bears finally defeated the Bulls and ran off with the honor until 1939. Captain J.W. Peavy scored the highest of the 9 Captains. Captains Page, Mayo, and Peavy won places in the race for National Emblem Club Pins. The School Division under the leadership of Lanier and Spivey presented the best record in the history of the School Division. The Industrials lead by Jordan and Mayo in collaboration with the Ship Channel Battalion came close to knocking the School Division out of gear. The Water Front Battalion under Freeman and Spiller and other channel leaders brought in 327 members. Drs. Beal and Parrott lead sustaining forces to victory lining up over 100 sustaining memberships. Armstead and Ponder's appeal to lodges, clubs, and organizations was also very successful.

TIMELINE 1938

June 25, 1938
Dr. Bethune Address Dover Grads

ILA Y Center Processing

Third Ward Y Center Popular

July 9, 1938
Houston College Summer School Holds Picnic

YMCA Elects New Management Group

Y Softball League

Second Y Camp for Boys at Spring, Texas will leave the Y Pilgrim Building July 11, 1938 at 8:30 am

Y Centers Enroll at nearby Y

July 16, 1938
Men's Day at Trinity East is A Success

Y Softball Notes
Social Division All Stars defeated the Industrial Division All Stars in a twin bill before 2,000 spectators on July 4, 1938 at Emancipation Park.

July 23, 1938
Y Camps to Close Saturday

July 30, 1938
Rosenwald Fund Names Director and Trustees

August 20, 1938
Seventy Fifth Anniversary of Negro Freedom Saint Louis September 7-11, 1938

September 17, 1938
The YMCA physical department plans a Citywide Ping Pong Tournament

Reverend R.T. Bingham pastor of Mount Carmel Baptist Church conducting a one-day revival at True Light Baptist Church on Liveoak

Research suggests that the first Negro, Anthony Johnson, came to America as an indentured servant in 1618. After fulfilling his obligations, Johnson became a landowner and secured the services of John Casor. However, Johnson keep Casor in service seven years longer than the indenture called for and was released from servitude after the intervention of whites.

TIMELINE 1938

September 17, 1938
YMCA Elects Officers for the Coming Year

October 15, 1938
Jemison Leads Chamber Poll

Appoint School Officer

October 22, 1938
Julius Rosenwald Fund Offers Fellowships

The YMCA Moves On

November 12, 1938
YMCA to Conduct Prayer, Fellowship Week

Texas International Longshoremen

November 19, 1938
YMCA Golden Jubilee Meet Well Attended

Mary McLeod Bethune speaker

December 10, 1938
Negroes Win with GOP

The YMCA Summer Camp

The YMCA Summer Camp opened on July 1, 1938 with 60 boys attending session 1 under the leadership of Camp Director Sidney Smith, junior at the Meharry Medical College. Seven departments consisting of college students and past participants, Wendell Terrell, I.W. Kaffie, J.L. Blount, Jr., Joseph Harris, and Wendell Terrell, oversaw camp activities and supervision of nearly 200 campers from July 1-23, 1938. Terrell, Wheatley High School student, oversaw swimming. The summer camp reunion program and reenactments of camp scenes was held at the Pilgrim Building on July 29, 1938.

YMCA's Eight Annual Prayer Week Program

The YMCA conducted its Eight Annual Prayer Week Program November 13-20, 1938 at 47 locations throughout the city at local schools, the YMCA, Houston Belt and Terminal, SP Shops, main post office and all sub stations, Union Stations, Ship Channel under the leadership of Reverend J.S. Scott Chairman of the Religious Work Committee and 30 volunteers. The theme of the fellowship week was *Enrichment of Our Spiritual Lives by Meditation and Prayer*.

YMCA Elected Officers for 1939

William C. Craver Executive Secretary
F.L. Lane, Chairman
J.C. McDade, Vice President
James Charles Sanderson, Recording Secretary
R.A. Williams, Assistant Recording Secretary
Boys Work J.C. Sanderson
Education J.E. Armstead
Building Fund W.E. Miller
Socials and House R.A. Williams
Finance C.A. Shaw
Interracial James D. Ryan
World Service E.O. Smith
Physical Work E.L. Snyder
Membership Solon Brandon and J.H. Jemison Co Chairmen
Industrial Plants R.H. Guess
Railway Trainmen M.W. Jordan
James D. Ryan
W.E. Miller
Freeman Everett
T.M. Fairchild
J.S. Scott

New additions to the committee, Everett and Jemison, were Chairmen of the 1938 Spring Membership Campaign.

1939

The Colored YMCA 1939 Membership Campaign was the largest campaign executed. The Y conducted 213 committee meetings and 758 other meetings including classes, clubs, camps, athletic tournaments, hikes, religious meetings and conferences collectively serving 49,387 boys, women, and men. 6,000 men and boys had direct contact with the Y.

Emancipation Park

William Ward Watkins architect for the city of Houston buildings and grounds department announced the building of a $33,330 permanent structure at Emancipation Park (February 4, 1939).

Seventh Annual Father Son Banquet

The Y celebrated its Seventh Annual Father Son Banquet under the leadership of F.L. Lane, Branch Chairman and J.C. Sanderson, Chairman for the Boys Department. J.E. Gooden Father and Son Committee Chairman presided. The Keynote Speaker was Dr. J.G. Gathings and the Boys Keynote was Yates High School Student Cecil McGriff. The Boys chorus from Harper and Washington High School performed and Wheatley High School Orchestra rendered selections (March 4, 1939).

First Colored Army-Navy YMCA

On Sunday July 13, 1939, Columbus, Georgia opened the first Colored Army-Navy Branch of the Young Men Christian Association under the leadership of Mr. Thomas A. Ryker, head of the Army and Navy Work for the Y. The two-story brick structure with auditorium, social halls, game rooms, and temporary residence facilities was built to accommodate hundreds of Colored soldiers from New York and Southern Divisions. The Y building was erected according to YMCA

TIMELINE 1939

February 4, 1939
It was 76 years ago that honest Abe' freed the race

YMCA League all-star ballot

Army, navy gets first Y Branch

What To Do In An Air Raid

Rosenwald Day A Call to Prayer

February 5, 1939 will be a day of prayer for Negro people in America for the relief of the suffering of the victims of racial prejudice throughout the world.

February 11, 1939
Houston Hails Plan to erect YMCA Building in Houston
Gavin Ulmer president of the board of directors of the Houston Young men Christian association announced the YMCA campaign for a Building Fund of $1,375,000

February 25, 1939
Houston Behind in YMCA provision, building to fill need
The program will consist of a new modern downtown central building and Branch buildings for both white and Negro activities.

March 18, 1939
South Texas older boys conference to be at Beaumont
Texas 18th older boys conference at Beaumont March 31-April 2

Houston Y Drive is now underway
DeFrantz on scene

March 25, 1939
Drake to head Y Drive

April 1, 1939
Y Drive Forces Complete

April 8, 1939
Nation's Eyes Focused on Local Y Drive
Citizens far and near herald plan for Y building here

April 15, 1939
Colored Division sets $50,000 as a goal in Building Fund Drive

standards with funding from private investors and leased to the YMCA.

Special Membership

On Friday October 20, 1939, the Y's special membership roll call and renewal of members got underway with more than 50 solicitors taking the field under the leadership of General Chairman A.R. Turner and Associate General Chairman W.C. Denson.

9th Annual YMCA Setup Conference

The Y held its 9th Annual YMCA Setup Conference of the committee of management and its subcommittee at the Y auditorium assembly room in the Pilgrim Building Friday night on September 29, 1939 at 8pm. The address was delivered by W.L. Davis and A.R. Turner to Head Y Parley.

TIMELINE 1939

April 15, 1939
Baptists Endorse Y Drive

YMCA Softball Notes
The first time out this season the Houston Heights and Star Drugs teams are providing strong teams.

April 22, 1939
Y Workers Get Points On Campaign
In a coaching meeting E.L. Snyder gave points for a successful salesmanship to three divisions-U, V, and W headed by Phillip Page, J.E. Gooden, and John Codwell.

On Tuesday night 60 officers of the campaign in a dinner meeting saw the movie the Negro and the YMCA.

150 Workers to Take Field in Y Drive Monday

Big Y Campaign for $1,375,000 is on! The Colored Division out for $50,000

Three divisions of workers to comb field
- Drake and associates confident
- Special gifts directed by Chas A. Shaw
- Team organization Frank Lane

Every worker is on fire sigh the idea that *we can, we must, we will secure our goal and the erection of a $185,000 building*

April 29, 1939
Workers in Y Drive Hit the Field

Softball League Standings
Joes place split a double header with the Trojans 9-10

April 29, 1939
Seventy-five out of town and local speakers told the story of the work of the YMCA

New Proposed YMCA Building for Negroes

The new proposed YMCA building for Negroes in Houston, Texas would be the 26th modern YMCA building constructed for Negroes with a minimum cost of $185,000 for construction. During the period of April 24-May 4, 1939, a Building Fund Drive of $1,375,000 was sought for modern Downtown Central Building and Branch buildings for both white and Negro activities.

The Colored YMCA Building Fund Committee under the leadership of Campaign Director Dr. Robert B. DeFrantz was composed of 20 teams who were in the field as special boosters of pledge paying on the part of Negro subscribers to the proposed $185,00 Negro Y Building upon which construction was projected to begin as soon as the Negro citizens paid a sufficient amount, $50,000, to warrant the approval of the Association's General Director to begin erecting the structure with club rooms and swimming pool. The YMCA's City General Building Fund Campaign for $1,375,000 was unanimously endorsed by the Houston Baptist Ministers Association in their regular meeting. A statement of the campaign's progress for the new Colored Y building was made by William C. Craver and the Reverend and Ministers Association President L.H. Simpson.

The names of all the men and women who subscribed and completed their payments to the new YMCA's Building Fund to be built for Colored men and boys of Houston would be deposited in the cornerstone of the new building during the

TIMELINE 1939

May 13, 1939
Negroes Pass Goal In Y Building Drive Extended To May 22
The division topped $52,000 in subscriptions

Managers Phillip Page and William Sweeney Division U turned in $4,873 cash and pledges

Managers J.E. Gooden and J.W. Peavy Division V $5,783 cash and pledges

Managers John Codwell and Theo H. Thompson Division W $6,215

Chairman Chas A. Shaw Special Gifts Committee $39,474

Codwell and Thompson were crown Kings in Leadership securing cash and pledges for their division

July 8, 1939
Three-Way Tie In Y Softball Loop

July 22, 1939
Houston Y Will Be 26th For Larger Centers

future cornerstone ceremony. Subscriptions ranged from $5 to $10,001. Prior to the Building Fund Kickoff, T.M. Fairchild, J.A. Fowlkes, James D. Ryan, and E.O. Smith sent invitations to over 500 people asking for subscriptions. The men invited the Colored National YMCA Secretary W.H. Hunton to attend the Campaign Kickoff in April 1939. Seventy-five out of town and local speakers told the story of the work of the Young Men's Christian Association not only among Colored men and boys but among thirty-six nations of the world. Fifty pastors preached on the challenge of youth or spoke on adding words of encouragement to their congregations to help in the building of $185,000 YMCA plan outlined in the new Y program of expansion for the city of Houston.

The Colored YMCA Building Fund Committee
- Dr. Drake, General Chairman
- Church Cooperation Committee W.L. Davis Chairman and Reverend J.S. Scott Associate Chairman
- Prospects Committee J.C. Sanderson Chairman
- Public Relations Chairman J.E. Armstead
- Solon Brandon Associate Chairman
- Industrial Groups M.W. Jordan And R.H. Guess Co-Chairmen
- Arrangements J.H. Jemison Chairman
- R.A. Williams Associate Chairman
- Group Contacts E.L. Snyder Chairman
- The Citizens' Advisory Committee W.E. Mille Lane Chairman of Organizations in the Y Drive
- T.M. Fairchild, J.A. Fowlkes, James D. Ryan, and E.O. Smith

TIMELINE 1939

August 5, 1939
Y Softball Tourney Announced

Dates Announced For Y Softball Tourney Gross Clouts No. 3

Y Opens Bank For Campers

August 19, 1939
Calhoun Pitches Bats Skippers To Houston Y Title
Southpaw Calhoun pitched and batted the ILA Skippers to Victory in the YMCA softball tournament by defeating Atlanta Life 6-2.

September 23, 1939
Annual YMCA Setup Conference Slated For Houston Branch

Theme forward with the branch program.

YMCA membership at the colored branch surpasses all previous enrollments

The 1938-39 total membership enrollment for the branch men and boys 3,787...increase in 300 members from the sections of the city where Neighborhood Works is being carried out by the branch.

Houston Y Camp Largest in Southwest-500 boys have been trained in swimming, scouting, and drilling during the summer months Spring Creek

September 30, 1939
W.L. Davis and A.R. Turner to Head Y Parley

New Y building site to be selected soon

October 21, 1939
Y workers to kick off Friday seek renewals

Annual Julius Rosenwald Memorial
On February 4, 1940, the Colored YWCA and YMCA presented the Annual Celebration of Life Memorial for Julius Rosenwald at Bebee Tabernacle. The annual celebration was a tribute to Julius Rosenwald's life. According to Dr. C.H. Tobias, General Secretary of the Negro Movement, Rosenwald was the greatest benefactor of the Negro since Abraham Lincoln. The event speakers for the glorious occasion were Dr. Paul W. Quillian, Pastor of the First Methodist Church and Reverend L.S. White, Pastor of Bebee Tabernacle Church.

Ninth Annual Older Boys Conference
The Colored YMCA held its Ninth Annual Older Boys Conference for South Texas in Galveston, Texas on March 23, 1940. Professor L.C. Phillips, Prairie View College, and D.N. Howell, Boys Work Director Moorland Branch YMCA, Dallas were the outstanding conference leaders and James Tucker of Wheatley High School was elected the 1940-41 President of the Conference. The conference also voted to send a delegate to the National Hi Y Conference held in Oberlin, Ohio June 20-24, 1940. The 20th annual conference was scheduled to be held in Corpus Christi upon the invitation of the High School and Chamber of Commerce.

Membership Campaign
The Colored YMCA launched its Tenth Annual Inclusive YMCA Membership Campaign on April 28, 1940. Directors of the Membership Department were L.J. Mann and R.H. Guess. The campaign was led by General Chairman J.E. Codwell, and Assistant Chairmen Dr. John W. Davis and Don Robby.

Division Managers
Thomas Parr Manager Division A and Jerome Busbee Manager Division B

J.C. Sanderson, Chairman of Special Gifts
William Ponder, Chairman Club Section
J.M. Mayo, Manager of Industrial Groups
Dean J.D. Bowels, Manager of the School Division
L.H. Spivey, Assistant Manager School Division
F.W. Logan, Chairman Church Cooperation
Freeman Everett, Leader of the Water Front Groups

The YMCA Tenth Annual Membership Campaign was the first Spring Membership Campaign since 1938 marking the last campaign under the Community Type of YMCA Work due to the fact that the new YMCA would require a new plan of

TIMELINE 1940

January 20, 1940
YMCA basketball league on the way

January 27, 1940
State Conference Director William Craver, Executive Secretary of the Houston Colored YMCA called together a committee to plan the Texas State Older Boys Conference

February 25-March 1, 1940
8th Annual Father and Son Observance Week

April 6, 1940
A committee of seven ministers lead by Reverend F.W. Logan are assisting Y leaders in the 1940 Membership Campaign

Jax Trojans Softball team will participate in the YMCA softball league

April 13, 1940
Houston Y league gets a flying start with serval of the major teams starting off strong especially Atlanta Life and Biltmore Cleaners

April 27, 1940
Y Membership Drive Gets Underway with John Codwell at the Helm

April 28-May 15, 1940
YMCA launch 10th Annual Spring Membership Drive

May 11, 1940
Atlanta Life still has clean slate in Y soft ball loop

May 18, 1940
Tenth Annual Membership Campaign

membership.

The Campaign surpassed its membership goals by signing up over 700 paid members with cash totaling $1,000. Over thirty men won red, silver, gold, and double Gold Star degrees in the Royal Order of Spizzerinktum. Outstanding captains were S.E. Riley, L.H. Cotton, and Fred Marshall. The Campaign's highest honor, the National Emblem Club pins worn by only eight men in Houston, was won by F.H. Purnell and S.E. Riley.

Building Fund

William C. Craver and the Board of Management recommend that the Y purchase the property at Gray and Hutchins for the new proposed Y Building. The purchase was approved by the Branch's Negro Building Committee C.A. Shaw, W.E. Miller, and Freeman Everett on June 1, 1940. *Observers say that the site for the building is one of the choicest and most prominent spots in the city. Transport line coverage at this point, downtown stores, post office and railway stations are easily accessible.*

On July 20, 1940, the Y announced that the Board of Directors of the Central Association needed the Colored Division to raise an additional $10,000 plus the amount already collected by September 1, 1940 in order to break ground for the new building.

In an effort to secure the required amount to begin construction on the new building, P.H. Holden developed a strategic strategy to visit 250 large donors in the campaign who total subscriptions amounted to $39,000 for additional funds so that beginning work on the new facility could begin early in September.

On September 6-8, 1940, the Employed Officers and YMCAs of Texas, Oklahoma and Arkansas Southwest Area Council YMCA celebrated its third annual meeting in Glenn Rose, Texas. Seventy-five secretaries and 10 Negro secretaries attended. William C. Craver was the chairman of the Colored Secretarial Group.

On Monday night, October 21, 1940, the YMCA held its Annual Honor and Award Night. Winning teams and individuals in recent membership Campaigns and athletic tournaments were awarded emblem pins, stars, and silver loving cup. The big features of the evening were speeches, songs, and yells lead by the Physical Committee chairmen J.E. Codwell and Odie Davis and the Membership Department R.H. Guess and L.J. Mann.

November 1-4, 1940 was set aside for Pledgers to the new Negro Y Building to pay their pledge. One thousand five hundred and

TIMELINE 1940

June 18
Balloting of softball got underway for the third annual industrial and social division all-star YMCA softball league which will be held in Sportsman Park
June 19

Thus, Social Division
L.A. Skippers, W.H.C. Products, Houston Heights, Weingarten Washington Hi-Y, Wheatley Hi Y Hughes Tools, Lori I, I.S. Lewis

Industrial Division
Atlanta Life, Obie's Southern Select, Jax Trojans, Club Memo Third Ward Stars, Starcor, Sealy Mattress, Star Drug, Club Matinee

July 20, 1940
$10,000 needed by September 1st to start work on Y Building
Three-way tie in both Divisions of softball Loop

August 3, 1940
Y Building Fund Committee to visit 250 in Drive
Y to steer boys work for August

August 10, 1940
Y Building Fund Committee in Collection Drive
Y Building will start as soon as sufficient funds are on hand
ILA, Club Memo Lead Y League

August 17, 1940
Y secretaries to meet at Glenn Rose

August 24, 1940
Fast entry makes YMCA tournament a virtual toss up

YMCA championship softball tournament starts Tuesday, August 27 at 7pm in Sportsman Park

eighty persons subscribed more than $60,000 to the fund and by October 26, 1940; 400 had completed payments. The largest subscribers were longshoremen locals 872, 1271, 1409, and 1525 cooperation with subscriptions totaling $4,000. Leadership making its subscriptions good were Freeman Everett, W.C. Denson, Jeff Robins, Leon Croney, John Burt, Elmo Gregory, John Fowlkes; A.R. Spiller, C.O. Jones, Ned Weathers and others.

The Y conducted a Special Campaign April 22 through May 19, 1941 to collect funds raised through subscriptions in The Negro Building Fund to hasten work on the new Negro Y Building. Only $20,000 pleaded had been paid in full as of March 29, 1941 resulting in the Board of Management of the Negro Branch electing Professor P.H. Holden, Principal of Burrus School, to act as General Chairman of the Building Fund Campaign of 1939.

P.H. Holden General Chairman
Reverend J.S. Scott Heads the Executive Committee
J.E. Gooden directs the organizations and teams

The Church Cooperation Committee was headed by Reverend S.A. Pleasants, Jr. cooperating with ministers who formed the church committee: Reverend A.A. Lucas, Reverend L.H. Simpson, Reverend L.S. White, Reverend T.J. Clement, Reverend L.C. Thomas, Reverend S.D. Stevens, Reverend J. Cook, Reverend J.H. Boyce, Reverend J.S. Lewis, Reverend J.D. Moore, Reverend John Gamble, and others.

Y Publicity Committee to inform citizens of the situation regarding the Building status was headed by Solon Brandon. Associated with Brandon were Carter Wesley, C.F. Richardson, C.W. Rice, B.M. Jackson, Henry Grayson, J.C. McDade, John L. Blount, Jr., Albert White, Jeff Robbins, and L.L. Lockhart

National Council Challenge

President W.R. Banks asked Negro leaders of the Southwest interested in the improvement of boys to help raise one thousand dollars to meet the challenge of the National Council which offered two thousand dollars six hundred to the group if the Texas Negroes raised one thousand dollars to help employ a full-time secretary to work among the colleges for the YMCA.

The following leaders pleaded contributions to the fund: President M.W. Dogan of Wiley College, President J.J. Rhoads of Bishop College, and Principal H.B. Pemberton of Marshall

TIMELINE 1941

November 9, 1940
YMCA Building Fund Committee to Report Monday

Big Y Building Fund Rally
December 1-6
YMCA calling all the 1,240 subscribers who have not yet finished payment on their pledges

November 23, 1940
Morehouse President to attend YMCA Institute at PV

December 7, 1940
Longshoremen largest subscribers to YMCA Building Fund

Leadership making its subscriptions good

December 14, 1940
YMCA Building Fund Honor Roll

January 18, 1941
Prayer Week 1941
Religious department led by Reverend J.S. Scott executed programs at 29 industrial, school, and church centers serving 7,000 men, boys, and women

Summer Camp for Boys at Spring, Texas YMCA planning to improve the camps roads, at athletic fields, increase the size of the kitchen and dining services, and to serve no fewer than 500 boys during summer camp.

The colored YMCA increases from 3 Y clubs in 1932 to 30 in 1940. 40 sponsors. L.K. Shivery and C.C. Mack supervise the boys' programs

4th release of YMCA honor roll for new YMCA building fund

February 8, 1941
YMCA building committee holds meeting first 20 days of January $700 cash is collected.

Pledged $100 for Marshall, Principal R.T. Tatum fifty for Beaumont, President J.W. Yancy II of Paul Quinn promised to make a contribution for Paul Quinn and Waco President Mary E. Branch of Tilloston promised fifty for Tillotson and Austin, Professor Frank Windom fifty dollars for Galveston; Dr. G.L. Harrison President of Langston University pledged $100 for Oklahoma; President M.I. Harrison Philander Smith College promised that Arkansas will come in with its share.

On December 6-8, 1940, Dr. Benjamin E. Mayes President of Morehouse College Atlanta Georgia lead conference discussions at the Y Leadership Institute Prairie View College.

Four sections of the Big Y Drive for Building Funds met on Sunday, May 4, 1941 at 3pm as one army at the Colored YMCA in room 305, Pilgrim Temple with the main objective to recruit 98 volunteers to call upon more than 1,200 prospects in order to raise $12,000 cash to ensure the beginning of work on the new YMCA building.

On Wednesday, June 30, 1941, the President of the Julius Rosenwald Fund Edwin R. Embree, announced Rosenwald Fellowship Awards of 64 fellowships totaling $100,000. Forty Negroes and 24 white southerners were selected out of over 500 applicants to receive fellowships averaging $1,500. The awards were made in two categories: to Negroes in any field and from and part of the United States, and to white Southerners who wish to work on some problem distinctive to the South, and who expect to make their career in that region.

The YMCA Special Drive for Y Building campaign workers voted unanimously at the fourth report meeting of the Building Fund Collection on May 12, 1941 to continue the drive among subscribers until June 2, 1941.

Special Gifts Leadership
Chairman P.H. Holden
3 Division Leaders: Managers McDade, Harris, and Mann
Captains: Solomon, C.W. Hicks, Doyle Branch, Chiles Washington, P. Brantley, L.H. Cotton, T.H. Parr, W.L.D. Johnson, Jr., R.C. Grier, F.H. Purnell, D. Johnson, and others

The YMCA softball council donated proceeds from the gala affair for the All Star Game held on July 4, at Sportsman Park to the YMCA Building Fund.

The Colored YMCA reorganized and voted to continue collections of 1,075 scribers Building Fund Pledges during the

TIMELINE 1941

February 8, 1941
P.H. Holden re-elected chairman of the committee for the next 90 days J.H. Jemison assistant J.E. Armstead leaders of the Wildcats/Division A. L.J. Mann leader of Bulldogs Division B

C.A. Shaw and W.E. Miller won the gold loving cup for collecting the largest amount of cash $677 Runner ups F.L. Lane and J.E. Goode

Medal went to team of David Williams and J.C. Calhoun Cats team. Solon Brandon and Dewey Roberts lead the wildcats in collections

March 1, 1941
Y Building Honor Roll
Over 300 names of persons who have completed payments on their subscriptions ranging from $5 to $10,001. Building fund committee turns in cash collections of $600

March 1, 1941
Dragging and Still Lead Y Loop
The catholic dragons continued their winning stride at Emancipation Park and defeated the YMCA Red Raiders for the municipal cage title.

March 29, 1941
Y to Conduct Campaign for Funds on Building

April 5, 1941
Y To sponsor two softball leagues

First Round Played in YMCA tourney

The YMCA's preseason softball tournament for the entering Y Industrial and Social Leagues start on April 6.

April 12, 1941
Y Building Fund Grow Daily
The film the New Colored YMCA is being shown in all Houston Theatres

summer months. Approximately 500 scribers completed payments out of a total of 1,575.

William C. Craver, Executive Secretary, announced on August 9, 1941 that the Board of Directors of the Central YMCA concurred with a nominating committee of the Colored Branch YMCA in the appointment of 21 men to constitute the Committee of Management of the Association for 1941-42. The men appointed to conduct Branch affairs and programs were Armstead, Solon Brandon, Freeman Everett, T.M. Fairchild, R.H. Guess, P.H. Holden, F.L. Lane, J.E. M.W. Jordan, J.H. Jemison, L.J. Mann, W.E. Miller, J.C. McDade, Dr. C.W. Pemberton, C.A. Shaw, E.O. Smith, J.C. Sanderson, Reverend J.E. Scott, R.A. Williams, J.E. Gooden, F.H. Purnell, and J.E. Codwell. P.H. Holden was chosen as Chairman to succeed Frank L. Lane. Lane resigned after 10 years of service on the Building Fund Committee and over six years leadership as Branch Chairman.

F.C. Fields, the General Secretary of the YMCA, sent E.O. Smith, T.M. Fairchild, Frank L. Lane, M.W. Jordan, and R.A. Williams a special letter praising them for their long and faithful years of service to the Colored YMCA.

P.H. Holden presided over the first Committee Management meeting of the year electing J.C. McDade as Vice Chairman, J.C. Sanderson, Recording Secretary, R.A. Williams, Assistant Secretary. Chairman Holden appointed the following men to serve as Chairman of Departments for the year: F.L. Lane, Finance, J.C. McDade, Boys Work, Dr. C.W. Pemberton, Employment and Relief, J.E. Gooden, World Service, W.E. Miller, New Building, C.A. Shaw, Personnel, L.J. Mann and F.H. Purnell, Membership, M.W. Jordon, Inter-church Relations, J.S. Scott, Religion, J.H. Jemison, Socials and Entertainments, J.E. Goodwell, Physical programs, Solon Brandon, Campus and Hikes, J.E. Armstead, Education, Freeman Everett and R.H. Guess, Industrial Relations, E.O. Smith, Interracial Problems.

L.J. Mann and F.H. Purnell, Membership Directors, were authorized to conduct a Membership Campaign during October and November to recruit new members and renew five hundred men and three hundred boys' memberships that expired in May.

The committee also appointed a group to re-study and set in motion plans to have the new Y Building erected at an early date.

W.C. Craver, Executive, L.K. Shivery, Boys Work Secretary, and C.C. Mack, Director of Athletic Activities attended the conferences of Employed Officers of the YMCA's of Southwest

TIMELINE 1941

May 3, 1941
Rosenwald Fellowship Awards are announced

Y softball league gets underway

May 17, 1941
Special Drive for Y Building to Continue

Observance of 75th Year of Freedom was held at Emancipation Park. Students from Houston College for Negroes read the Emancipation Proclamation.

May 31, 1941
Y Building Campaign to Make final report-The Negro YMCA Building Fund Campaigners will make their final report on Monday night June 2, 1941 at 6:30 pm.

June 14, 1941
Y Building Fund Collectors to Make Report-The Negro YMCA Building Fund Campaigners will make their final report on Monday night Wednesday, June 18, 1941 at 7 pm.

July 12, 1941
Proceeds from game going to Y Building Fund

July 19, 1941
Y to Collect Building Funds During Summer

August 9, 1941
Managing Board is named to plan Y Work

September 6, 1941
Community Chest Gets off with a bang

September 20, 1941
Y Organizes for the Year

Conference is attended by Y Staff

Area of The National YMCA. Seventy-Five Secretaries and Associations were in attendance and the Negro issue was squarely put up to the secretaries and their boards.

The Negro Child Center, unmarried mothers, YMCA, YWCA, Negro Hospital, Boy Scouts, Tuberculosis Clinic and Visiting Nurses Association received a portion of the $65,000 raised by the Chest Drive.

General Chairman T.H. Henderson assisted by Associate Chairman J.M. Calhoun announced the Leaders of the Bulls and Bears division for the YMCA Membership Campaign November 14-December 2, 1941. The leader of the Bulls were S.E. Riley and Dewey Roberts while the Bears leaders were Odie Davis and R.H. Moore. The three Divisions were tasked with calling 1,000 prospects during the campaign which started on November 6, 1941.

Men and Mission Day

The YMCA observed Men and Mission Day on Sunday, November 30. There were laymen from 75 churches of all denominations invited to attend the meeting and participate. The meeting was held under the auspices of the Ministers Interdenominational Alliance and Young Men's Christian Association. Reverend J.S. Scott, Chairman of the Alliance and W.C. Craver, Executive Secretary of the YMCA.

The Sixth Annual YMCA Institute

The Sixth Annual YMCA Institute with William C. Craver presiding was held at Prairie View State College on December 5-7 under the auspices of the Southwest Area Council of the YMCA Work Committee. One hundred twenty-six secretaries, sponsors, and general workers attended the conference. Dr. J.L. Horace of the Monumental Baptist Church of Chicago, Illinois was the keynote speaker. The conference theme was *Rethinking Our Task-The Philosophy; Problems and Program of the YMCA*.

Reverend W.O. Gill Professor of Religion of Jarvis College Hawkins Texas conducted the devotion in the second session and Dr. Horace made an address on *Seeking Our Goal* in the third session, the most important session.

Christmas Week

During Christmas Week, under the leadership of J.H. Jemison, Chairman of the House and Social Affairs, the YMCA conducted

TIMELINE 1941

October 25, 1941
Open Drive for New Members

November 8, 1941
Fourth Ward Chest team raises quota

Name Leaders in the Y Drive

November 15, 1941
Y to Observe Mission. Day

December 13, 1941
Prairie View is Host to Annual YMCA Institute

Y Building Fund Leaders to Push Drive to Close

December 27, 1941
T.M. Fairchild prominent citizen of Houston dies
1114 St Emmanuel Street

Y Building Fund Leaders to Push Drive to Close

YMCA to have tree for needy

Chairman P.H. Holden will launch an intense effort beginning in 1942 to bring to a successful culmination the plans for the new Negro Y building. Nearly half the money pledged is in hand and pledges still coming in.

The 4 men who pledged $1,000 or more pledged are in and a large number who have pledged $500 or more are also in.

a Christmas program and tree for needy Negro boys. The boys of the Camp Saving Club planned the program with assistance of L.K. Shivery and C.C. Mack on December 19, 1941.

World War II

On December 27, 1941, Holden stated that the fact that we are plunged into a long and frightful war makes the need for a new facility more urgent. However, the campaign was haunted by World War II. Research estimates that during World War II over 2.5 million African American men registered for the draft, and large numbers of African American women volunteered to serve in the Army, Army Air Forces, Navy, Marine Corps, and Coast Guard. Over 50 countries fought on the battlegrounds of Asia, Europe, North Africa, the Atlantic and Pacific oceans, and the Mediterranean Sea in one of the world's most deadly and costliest wars in world history, World War II. The United States entered the war in 1941 after Japanese planes bombed Pearl Harbor, Hawaii on December 7, 1941.

References

25th Century Club Annual Meeting. Thursday, May 18, 1972. A Salute to Our Century Clubbers.

Bagby Street YMCA 1951 Annual Program. Bagby Street YMCA 1954 Annual Program.

Bagby Street YMCA 1955 Annual Program.

Dr. Charles Jackson, c. 1920s (Courtesy of Riverside General Hospital and Drs. Levi V. and Eula Perry).

Dr. Rupert O. Roett, c.1918 (Printed in Houston Informer, courtesy of Riverside General Hospital and Drs. Levi V. and Eula Perry).

DuBois, W.E.B. Memo to NAACP Spingarn Medal Letter, January 23, 1920).

Greater Houston Black Chamber Cornerstone at 2808 Wheeler Street.

Gruening, Martha. 1917. Houston An NAACP Investigation.

Jackson, Andrew Webster. 1938. A Sure Foundation & A Sketch of Negro Life in Texas.

Joel Weintraub transcriber from 1931-32 City Directory and 1940 Street Directory.

Johnson, K. and Waites, A. 1920. Two Colored Women: With the American Expeditionary Forces.

Mease, Quentin R. 2001. On Equal Footing. Eakin Press.

Nichols, Gary. 2011. YMCA of Greater Houston Archives #30.

Prairie View A&M University History and Traditions. Retrieved on July 15, 2018 from www.pvamu.edu.

RGH Riverside General Hospital History http://riversidegeneralhospital.org.

Scott Emmett J. 1919. The American Negro in the World War. Chapter XXVIII. Chicago Homewood Press.

The Gregory School. 2019. http://www.thegregoryschool.org/library.html.

The Houston Informer (Houston, Texas) Saturday, July 17, 1920.

The Houston Informer (Houston, Texas) Saturday, November 27, 1920.

The Houston Informer (Houston, Texas) Vol 2, No. 52, Ed.1 Saturday, May 14, 1921 page:1 of 8.

The Houston Informer (Houston, Texas) Vol 4, No. 39, Ed. 1 Saturday, February 17, 1923 page:1 of 8.

The Houston Informer (Houston, Texas) Vol 4, No. 48, Ed. 1 Saturday, April 21, 1923 page:1 of 10.

The Houston Informer (Houston, Texas) Vol 5, No. 21, Ed. 1 Saturday, October 13, 1923 page:5 of 8.

The Houston Informer (Houston, Texas) Vol 5, No. 39, Ed. 1 Saturday, February 16, 1924 page:1 of 8.

The Houston Informer (Houston, Texas). January 1-December 31, 1918-1947.

The Houston Informer (Houston, Texas), January 1-December 31, 1948-1950.

The Pilgrim Building Alumni Reunion Reception Program. November 25, 1995.

The Pittsburgh Courier Pittsburgh, Pennsylvania. Saturday, June 16, 1928 page 14.

The Pittsburgh Courier Pittsburgh, Pennsylvania. Saturday, February 18, 1939 page 22.

The Pittsburgh Courier Pittsburgh, Pennsylvania. Saturday, June3, 1939 page 22.

The Pittsburgh Courier Pittsburgh, Pennsylvania. Saturday, December 11, 1943 page 13.

The Pittsburgh Courier Pittsburgh, Pennsylvania. Saturday, February 12, 1944 page 12.

The Pittsburgh Courier Pittsburgh, Pennsylvania. Saturday, January 4, 1947 page 14.

The Pittsburgh Courier Pittsburgh, Pennsylvania. Saturday, January 25, 1947 page 14.

The Pittsburgh Courier Pittsburgh, Pennsylvania. Saturday, February 15, 1947 page 18.

The Pittsburgh Courier Pittsburgh, Pennsylvania. Saturday, March 1, 1947 page 14.

The Pittsburgh Courier Pittsburgh, Pennsylvania. Saturday, June12, 1948 page 12.

The Pittsburgh Courier Pittsburgh, Pennsylvania. Saturday, August 13, 1949 page 20.

The Pittsburgh Courier Pittsburgh, Pennsylvania. Saturday, June12, 1951 page 12.

The Pittsburgh Courier Pittsburgh, Pennsylvania. Saturday, March 29, 1952 page 18.

The Red Book of Houston (Houston: Sontex Publishing Company, circa 1915).

www.ingramcontent.com/pod-product-compliance
Lightning Source LLC
Chambersburg PA
CBHW080415170426
43194CB00015B/2822